BULIMIA S*CKS!

10 SIMPLE STEPS TO STOP BINGEING & PURGING

Kate Hudson–Hall, Dip. AdvHYP (NSHAP)

Bulimia Sucks! 10 Simple Steps to Stop Bingeing & Purging

Copyright © 2020 Kate Hudson-Hall

The resources in this book are provided for informational purposes only and should not be used to replace the specialized training and professional judgment of a health care or mental health care professional.

ISBN: 978-1-8382381-0-0

DEDICATION

This book is dedicated to...

My father, whom I never knew and my loving mother, wherever she may be! If it weren't for both, this book would never have materialized.

Alan, for your guidance, inspiration, and motivation to write this book.

For my three and a half musketeers - my sons, Luca, Tino, and Lorenzo, who have supported my ramblings! Plus, a bonus—my funny and incredibly talented granddaughter, Lila Rose.

**As a huge thank you for investing in my book,
I have created you a:**

FAMILY & FRIENDS SUPPORT EBOOK DOWNLOAD

So, when you are ready for that help and encouragement from
your loved ones, download and send them the mini ebook
to learn positive tips to support you in your recovery.

**CLICK HERE TO SIGN UP FOR YOUR FREE FAMILY &
FRIENDS SUPPORT EBOOK DOWNLOAD**

https://bulimiasucks.com/support-e-book/

PLUS THERE'S MORE...

A DYNAMIC BULIMIA SUCKS! HYPNOSIS RECORDING DOWNLOAD

This powerful relaxation hypnosis recording will guide your
unconscious mind to reprogram your bulimic behaviors so that
you will change the way you are thinking and feeling and
motivate you towards your goal of freedom from bulimia.

It's best to listen to this recording when you have
40 minutes to relax, let go and allow your unconscious
mind to absorb all the powerful suggestions. Enjoy!

**WARNING: Please do not listen to this recording while driving, operating
heavy machinery, or if you have epilepsy or clinical depression.**

**CLICK HERE TO DOWNLOAD YOUR FREE POWERFUL MP3
BULIMIA SUCKS! HYPNOSIS DOWNLOAD**

https://bulimiasucks.com/bulimia-recording/

"SOMETIMES WHEN YOU ARE FEELING LONELY, DESPERATE AND SUBMERGED, YOU THINK YOU'RE DROWNING, BUT YOU CAN ACTUALLY BEGIN TO GROW WATER WINGS, BECAUSE NOW IS YOUR TIME TO LEARN TO SWIM"

KATE HUDSON-HALL

PROLOGUE

It was Christmas Day, the beginning of my road to recovery. I was terrified of not staying in control of all my triggers, urges, binges, purges, guilt, shame, disgust and everything else that will be piled onto my tinsel adorned dinner plate. Twelve of us perched around the festive table. With plenty of entertainment as I ate.

I wasn't listening; the anxiety in me had begun to rise. I knew my mother had one eye on me, watching my every mouthful as I finished my enormous plate of Christmas fodder—well, it wasn't, but that's how it looked to me. My sadness was rising as I became more focused on how much I had eaten rather than enjoying my Christmas.

I had been careful with the amount of food I had eaten, but not careful enough. I was beginning to feel a little too full as the anxiety continued to rise. With the persistent whispering negative thoughts intensifying, the tension tightened. The guilt of overeating, having food in my stomach, continued to build. The escalating shame of what I was about to do caused my anxiety to grip me so tightly that I could hardly breathe. The whispering in my head suddenly became deafening.

I couldn't take it anymore. With fear seeping from every pore, I slipped away from the table, tripping over my panic as I rushed to the bathroom. I gripped the handle of the door. It was locked.

I could hear laughter coming from the Christmas festivities. With blind panic, I scrabbled up the stairs towards the second bathroom, my hysteria squeezing my anxiety.

I'd made it to the top and skedaddled down the corridor towards the bathroom; my relief was in sight now. With sweaty palms, I seized the handle. Oh my God, it was jammed. I threw myself against the door. It was padlocked; there was no way in. The pain was too much as I collapsed into a heap. I was about to die.

I suddenly jumped, awaking from another nightmare back into my very own living bulimia infused nightmare.

Unfortunately, this dream is a perfect example of what people with bulimia experience regularly, and it is very distressing.

CONTENTS

INTRODUCTION

**"NOW IS THE TIME TO SAVE THE LIFE YOU
ARE ENTITLED TO LIVE" —KATE HUDSON-HALL**

HOW TO USE THIS BOOK

Regardless of where you are in your recovery, this is where you need to start! What I would suggest is to read through the whole book, so you can begin to have a clearer picture of where you are now and what you need to think about to start your recovery.

If you haven't also purchased the accompanying Bulimia Sucks! workbook, buy a hardback notebook to use throughout each step. Then go right back to Step 1 and slowly work through each critical step and:

- Begin to understand what you need to do to start changing your behaviors.
- Learn each powerful technique thoroughly to change your patterns and habits, links, and negative behaviors.

Imagine unraveling your bulimia behavior and having the tools to rearrange them and then piece them back together, so they work effectively for you.

It's fantastic; you're here, thinking about where you are now and how you can move forward positively. Are you ready to make tremendous discoveries about yourself and learn to develop new powerful skills?

WARNING　　　　***IMPORTANT***　　　　***WARNING***

Suppose you're triggered by reading something in this book, and you feel like you want to slip back into your negative behavior. Then I want you to zip to Step 8, immediately and learn the EFT (Emotional Freedom Technique) before you do anything else to limit the difficult thoughts and feelings you may be having.

WARNING　　　　***CAUTION***　　　　***WARNING***

VIDEO DEMONSTRATION OF TECHNIQUES

Throughout the book, there are several techniques for you to learn and begin to change how you feel about different avenues to your bulimia.

It might help you to see these techniques in action to get a real grip on how to use them and to make sure you really hear what I am saying. At the end of each technique, you will find the link to the video demonstration so that you can click straight into action.

ICONS

You will find five icons repeated throughout the book. So, when you see these, I want you to pay attention.

 When you see this icon, please think of a positive phrase you can repeat to yourself to inspire your fire and propel your motivation forwards. For example: "I am learning how I can break free from bulimia permanently."

 When you see this icon, there will be a steaming hot tip for you to think about clearly.

 When you see this icon, if you have purchased the additional workbook, with empowering easy tables to complete, it's time to grab it and complete the exercise, otherwise, reach for your notebook and follow the instructions.

 When this icon pops up, oh yes, it's time for you to re-read and think about what you have learned.

 When you see this icon, it's time to be super proud of yourself; you will have completed a powerful technique.

"DON'T WAIT; THE TIME WILL NEVER BE 'JUST RIGHT.' START WHERE YOU STAND AND WORK WITH WHATEVER TOOLS YOU MAY HAVE AT YOUR COMMAND, AND BETTER TOOLS WILL BE FOUND AS YOU GO ALONG"—GEORGE HERBERT

HAVE YOU EVER WONDERED WHY YOU'VE GOTTEN INTO THESE COMPLICATED DESTRUCTIVE BULIMIC PATTERNS?

THE ANSWER IS:
LIMITING THE AMOUNT OF FOOD YOU EAT = LEADS YOU TO BULIMIA!

Understand that by restricting yourself from eating food, your body starts to panic and slips into doing whatever it can to keep you alive.

Think back to the start of your bulimia. Were you trying to lose weight? More than likely, this is the case. In the beginning, deciding you wanted to lose weight, you began limiting the amount of food your body needed. Continuously ignoring your hunger, you were driven to thinking about food all the time. Then the destructive pattern began.

As the cravings for food intensified, you then became so hungry you could eat a horse!

Then the urge to eat became uncontrollable, you binged on all the rich stodgy foods, and this overload of food then drove you to purge, freeing yourself of the enormous guilt because you were striving for that idyllic vision of a skinny you.

Some, after purging, feel a great "high." This is the only time they have a moment of brief calmness, which doesn't last long before the feelings of self-loathing, worthlessness or a multitude of other horrific emotions slither back into their mind, overriding all other thoughts in that confused mind.

Even though you know how damaging this is to your body and swear that you'll never do this again, in time, the thoughts and feelings again become too unbearable, and the whole cycle begins again; it becomes a habit and the "norm."

It all becomes too much, and you give up. But and this is a big, BUT you're reading this book for a reason, and by following the steps, you'll learn how to start to finally break free permanently.

ITS TIME TO CHANGE FROM THE INSIDE OUT

Now is the time to start to change from the inside out rather than outside in. Your recovery path free from bulimia is all about *change now*.

On the outside, you try to control your weight and eating patterns so you can feel good on the inside.

But now you need to learn to begin to address how you can feel good on the inside before you can even try to address all your challenging behaviors.

"YOU GET WHAT YOU FOCUS ON, SO CHANGE YOUR FOCUS AND YOU CAN CHANGE YOUR LIFE"

WHAT IS THE DIFFERENCE BETWEEN ANOREXIA AND BULIMIA?

Anorexia and bulimia are both eating disorders and are driven by the need to lose weight in an unhealthy and distorted pattern. They have many similar symptoms but exhibit different food-related behaviors. For example:

- People with anorexia drastically reduce the amount of foods eaten to lose weight.
- People with bulimia eat an excessive amount of food in a short time (binge) and then purge or take laxatives or diuretics to prevent weight gain.

Research shows us that approximately 50% of people who have anorexia develop bulimia or bulimic patterns, me included. I was a bundle of anorexia and bulimia, all intertwined into one massive mess.

Let's take a closer look at the different symptoms of both:

ANOREXIA NERVOSA ALSO KNOWN AS ANOREXIA

People with anorexia want to be as thin as possible. They stop eating or eat very little and have several emotional, physical and behavioral symptoms.

Examples of emotional symptoms are:

- An extreme fear of putting weight on or becoming fat
- Obsessed with their weight, dieting, and calories. They have a distorted body image and see themselves as much larger than reality
- Low self-esteem

Examples of physical symptoms are:

- Severe weight loss
- Dehydration
- Fatigue

- Fainting or dizziness
- Amenorrhea, or absence of menstruation

Examples of behavioral changes are:

- Skipping meals. A reduced amount of food and drink leads to very low weight
- Lying about how much food they've eaten
- Talking badly about their body
- Eating only certain "safe" foods, usually low calories foods
- Extreme exercising for long periods

BULIMIA NERVOSA ALSO KNOWN AS BULIMIA

Bulimia (boo-LEE-me-uh) is a serious, potentially life-threatening eating disorder. People with bulimia may secretly binge—eating large amounts of food with a loss of control over the eating—and then purge, trying to get rid of the extra calories in an unhealthy way.

To get rid of calories and prevent weight gain, people with bulimia may use different methods. For example, you may regularly self-induce vomiting or misuse laxatives, weight-loss supplements, diuretics, or enemas after bingeing. Or you may use other ways to rid yourself of calories and prevent weight gain, such as fasting, strict dieting, or excessive exercise.

If you have bulimia, you're probably preoccupied with your weight and body shape. You may judge yourself severely and harshly for your self-perceived flaws. Because it's related to self-image—and not just about food—bulimia can be hard to overcome. But effective treatment can help you feel better about yourself, adopt healthier eating patterns, and reverse serious complications. People with bulimia continue eating within their conditions. This behavior usually starts with a desire to be thinner. They binge large amounts of food and then purge to rid the body of the food (Mayo Clinic, n.d.).

There are different types of bulimia; so, let me explain further what they are:

Binge and purge bulimia

This is the most common type of bulimia in which people often appear to eat regularly or eat a large amount of food over a specific period, with a total lack of control during this period of binge eating. Then they force themselves to purge to stop themselves from gaining weight and to relieve themselves of food-related anxieties.

Non purging bulimia

Non purging bulimia is when people eat normally or overeat. But rather than purging to compensate for the foods eaten, they will do one or more of these:

- Excessively exercise
- Fast and stop eating for a day or more. (Bulimic fasting and weight-loss fasting have two different psychological and health implications. Dieters focus on food and weight, but with bulimics, **it's about so much more**. Yes, they focus on their weight and foods, but it's more about achieving a sense of control, numbing uncomfortable feelings, and earning praise or acknowledgment.)
- Abuse laxatives or diuretics
- Take laxatives and/or diuretics after a binge in an effort to lose weight and relieve emotional turmoil.

As with anorexia, many different emotional, behavioral, and physical symptoms can signal bulimia.

Examples of emotional symptoms are:

- An extreme fear of putting weight on or becoming fat
- Obsession with weight, dieting, and calories
- Poor body image. Seeing themselves as much larger than reality
- Low self-esteem

(People with bulimia are more likely to be of an average weight for their age group than those with anorexia.)

Examples of physical symptoms are:

- Weight fluctuates dramatically between 5 lbs to 20 lbs per week
- Callouses, sores, or scars on knuckles from regularly vomiting. Broken capillaries from repeated vomiting
- Puffy cheeks. Swollen lymph nodes
- Bloodshot eyes. Cracked lips due to dehydration
- Tooth decay and enamel erosion
- Gastrointestinal problems. Acid reflux

Examples of behavioral changes are:

- Skipping meals.
- Not wanting to eat in front of others
- Disappearing to the restroom after meals
- Never-ending worrying about their weight. Restricting calories or eating only certain "safe" foods, usually low calories foods

- Eating to the point of discomfort
- Extreme exercising for long periods, especially after they've eaten
- Being secretive or very focused on food

So, if you have bulimia, anorexia, or both, the knowledge you'll learn from reading this book will empower you to start addressing how you can move forward in your life, free from your eating disorder.

WHAT ABOUT MEN AND BULIMIA?

Anyone can develop bulimia. Bulimia doesn't discriminate according to your shape, size, age, race, ethnicity, gender, or income.

Most eating disorders are much more common in women and girls than in men and boys. Studies have shown that males accounted for roughly 10% of anorexia nervosa and bulimia nervosa eating disorder patients. With today's research, this percentage is much higher; although, statistics may not be accurate, as men tend to be more reluctant to look for help.

Some men don't recognize their symptoms as an eating disorder and don't reach out for help. Also, some men don't realize that their relationship with food affects other areas of their life or see that how they think and feel about themselves is causing their issues with food.

They aren't painfully thin and may think that men don't get eating disorders. But men have body issue challenges that can contribute to developing bulimia.

Many famous men have admitted to having bulimia, such as:

Elton John—We all know Elton!

Andrew Flintoff—Former England cricket captain

Richard Simmons—American fitness instructor and TV personality

Shane Dawson—American YouTube personality

Rory Bremner—British impressionist

And the list goes on.

Men develop bulimia for the same reason as women, but with added pressure.

Men appear to become bulimic for the same kind of reasons women do, with the added pressure to appear strong, independent, and in control.

Bulimia was only recognized as an eating disorder in its own right in 1979. So, there's still a stigma that surrounds any eating disorder, making it difficult for someone to get help. But it seems particularly difficult for men to admit they have an eating disorder, let alone reach out for support.

If you're a man with bulimia, asking for help isn't a sign of weakness, but incredible strength and courage. There's no shame in having bulimia. But avoiding looking for help could lead to severe, long-term health issues.

So, let's get talking about this and open up to how you're thinking and feeling. This book is for all the males out there with bulimia as well as the females.

Follow each step right through to the end and begin learning about what makes you tick and how you can free yourself from bulimia once and for all.

But before we get to the steps, I would first like to share my story with you.

MEMOIR

CHAPTER ONE: IN THE BEGINNING

Let me explain how my life unfolded into 15 years of bulimia nervosa.

My life began in an English town, Chesham. My very first memory is of me skipping out of the nursery at aged three, proudly clutching my very first creation, a colorful, glorious Easter egg basket. Oh yes, and what an exquisite basket it was. It wasn't the memory of one year before, when my father passed away from cancer of the esophagus!

With no memory of my father, childhood was good as far as I could recall with my one memory of my shining Easter basket.

Aged five I was off to school, which was an exceptionally traumatic time for me. With memories of the teacher dragging me, hysterical from the clutches of my mother's arms, and then leaving me to shiver, alone, at the glass door as I watched her, destitute and lonely, stumbling to her car. Secretly, she was more than likely excited as she sped off, finally free from the responsibility of her third child.

I now understand this was the beginning of my separation anxiety with my mother. This darn separation problem continued to intensify as I grappled through my childhood.

If we had more knowledge and understanding of why I felt this way, we could have reached out for help. But in the '60s, no one had a clue, and certainly not me!

The anxiety became so intense that I can recall taking tablets, presumably Paracetamol, to make myself ill and avoid school. I don't remember how many I took, but it worked; I stayed home from school!

It wasn't until I revealed to a friend my fantastic plan on how I could skip school and stay in my safe, secure, loving mother's arms that she then told her mother, and of course, the word spread like wildfire. Mother questioned me, and I, of course, denied it. Not believing me, she gave me a stern talking to, and nothing else came of it, apart from more school, of course.

I have two brothers, Rich and Mike, two years and six years my senior, respectively. They were great teasers. This was maybe a reflection of their own suffering, but being the younger sister, I was a prime target. They would always tease me that I was stupid, hopeless, useless, and ugly! Maybe I was ugly, but hey!

At age six, I was yanked out of the class for extra reading and spelling lessons. Standing up in front of the whole class, I was escorted out. Under one arm, I carried my weighty unintelligent seed and under the other was a large lump of humiliation.

The seed thought that I was stupid began to sprout. I thought people were right; I wasn't clever but stupid. Throughout my school life, these patterns continued to develop.

Teasing aside, as a nine-year-old, my life was good. Until my mother drove me over to a friend's house to play. Her parents weren't home on this particular day, and her 17-year-old brother was babysitting us. As she and I happily played with our beloved dolls, her brother burst into her room and invited us into his bedroom to listen to music.

Curiously following his friendliness, we skipped into his room. He slowly began purring, explaining how we were going to take turns and relieve him. *Relieve him of what?* I thought. Barking, he demanded I squat on his bed and perform oral sex while he molested me. Petrified, I followed his instructions knowing this didn't feel right. But he was a great beef, and I was a slither of a waif. What could I do?

I was relieved when it was all over. Turning to his sister, he then growled, "It's your turn." While I perched on a rickety old chair in shock, shivering at his demands, I watched.

Afterward, we returned to her bedroom and continued to play with our dolls! This happened several more times, and under his stern instruction, I never told a soul. I became cautious of going to their house.

Weighed down by my limiting belief that I was stupid, the seed had begun to thrive. Then at eleven, I was sent to prison. Well, that's how I remember it. But to others, it was called boarding school. My suitcase bulged, loaded with tuck, which are sweets to any reasonable person. In particular, I packed delicious Garibaldi biscuits, which I now liken to a flat piece of cardboard with squashed dead flies splattered throughout! Also, more than likely, a few clothes were thrown in for good measure.

With great sorrow, my mother drove me to my fate as I clutched my only real comfort from home, Tinkabell, my Koala bear. After a quick introduction, Mother was instructed to leave me with my new mother, the house mistress, who I later found out was an evil, immoral, wicked, ice maiden, also known as Ms. Delve.

I was assigned the bottom class of each subject, as teachers treated me as if I were stupid. My maths teacher resembled a stilettoed bean pole with a pointed nose. We could always hear her clip-clopping along to class. I'd be there shivering with nerves in anticipation of her evil teachings.

Unfortunately, she taught us for years, and one specific day she questioned me on what the area of a triangle was. Funnily enough, I was never good at geometry and had lost how to calculate areas when I was 7 years old. I had no clue what the answer was. So, she ended up humiliating me in front of the class for 25 minutes.

My punishment was to write out neatly the answer one thousand times. It worked! I still remember it to this day: multiply the base by the height and divide by two!

So, you see I wasn't stupid. I still remember it now! But this experience completed the cementing of my limiting belief. I wasn't good enough, intelligent enough, and I WAS stupid.

Sometimes, in the evenings, we were ravenous. Supper would be a biscuit or one small packet of crisps. Starving, I would sneak up to the dormitory when it was quiet. Rummage in the bottom of my locker. I would find my secret stash of Garibaldis.

At age 13, I had an experience that, now, being a therapist, was enlightening to me. At the time, at the annual sports day, it was like a miracle.

Usually, I was never chosen to participate in athletics. I wasn't good enough! There goes my limiting belief again! With great excitement, I found out that I had been selected to take part in the potato race! This involved homegrown sprouting potatoes lined up at different degrees. Eight girls had to race to pick up the first sprouting, then run back to base, place the bulbous beast on a shimmering tray. Then run forward to the next sprouting, grabbing the beauty as they raced back to base and so forth. In the practice run in the morning, as I slowly carried my negative belief that I was a failure, I slipped and dropped most of my sproutings. I was so disappointed. I came in last.

I had a friend who was a fantastic athlete who witnessed my embarrassment of slithering face down into the eye of a potato. She turned to me and explained what she always does before a run is to repeatedly tell herself, "I am going to win this race." I had nothing to lose, so I decided to give it a go.

As my event was announced, with great trepidation, I sheepishly lined up in my sprouting position after embedding the words of wisdom. The whistle blew, and I was like Usain Bolt on speed. Flying back and forth with my sproutings, I won the race. I couldn't believe it. I smashed it, potatoes and all. Oh yes, that incredible power of suggestion worked; I triumphed!

I mention this because it's a perfect example of how powerful visualization and goal setting can be. Giving your mind a more precise direction of what you want to achieve, you're so much more likely to accomplish your goal, which we'll discuss in Step 10.

I had set myself a goal—a clear vision of winning that race. I told myself that I was going to succeed. Therefore, I had much more of a chance at winning, rather than having a vision of me bumbling along, flapping, tripping, and coming in last. Without goals, you lack focus and direction, and in your recovery, setting clear and simple goals is a real key ingredient.

Our meals were held in the dining hall with massive paintings adorning the walls of posing ugly Victorian looking people. Many meals given were revolting—for example, cod in a white sauce that looked and tasted like flimsy fish bones hidden in murky pond water. The problem here was that if you didn't eat such a delight, then you would go hungry. Often, I would be at the ice maiden's table at lunchtimes, who would keep her evil sprouting eye on us to make sure our plates were empty.

If we didn't eat it all, she would sit and wait until we had finished, spitting a long lecture about food wastage, how ungrateful we were, and of course, the poor African children.

We could never complain because no one would listen. The ice maiden would discredit any goings-on, so we had to suffer.

CHAPTER TWO

Aged seventeen, I finally escaped the clutches of the ice maiden's prison. Freedom had never felt so empowering to anyone. Move over Nelson Mandala. This was real freedom! Having been locked away in a cage for the last seven years, I was finally allowed to breathe and begin to figure out life for myself.

My mother decided to sell the family house, move to Oxford, and get married to a chap called George, which I thought I was okay with. But in my 40s, I read my diary I'd written from age thirteen to seventeen. I found a page written in my 14-year-old, neatly composed script, disclosing how I felt about my mother dating George: "I hope Mummy never gets married to George. He's taking her away from me, and I feel so lonely. I have no one."

Lonely was how I felt most of my young life. But I don't remember feeling like this about George, as he became a father figure I never had. He was supportive, caring, and compassionate. I also acquired three irreplaceable step-brothers and a unique, entertaining step sister.

I moved to London on my own and started training to become a florist. That was a pathway that was thrust upon me, as my qualifications, after I left the highest achieving boarding school, were minimal.

I lived in a women's hostel for one year, near Marble Arch in London. I'd go to work, come back to the hostel, and just sit in the room. I was so unhappy and felt I had no one. I was even lonelier than at school. At least in the first prison, I made compassionate, supportive friends there. But in this situation, I knew no one, so these deserted, lonely feelings intensified. London or any big city can be isolating and an immensely lonely, solitary place. After that first year, I moved into a flat with a friend and remember thinking. *That was the worst year of my life.*

I gradually made a few friends at work and one of them tossed into the air the catastrophic suggestion: "If you eat a Mars bar and make yourself sick afterward, you won't put any weight on." I inhaled this with every pore in my body. Thus, the bulimic behavior began. Oh my, how powerful one suggestion can be.

Let me explain how these two horrific diseases, bulimia and anorexia, became intertwined in my life. I was a skinny bean but began to have a more curvy, shapely body. I felt I was developing into a porker, becoming slightly overweight, which I wasn't; I had just been a late developer.

So, I thought, *What better way to control this problem? I can eat what I want, then make myself sick, and not gain any weight! Marvellous, what an ingenious idea!*

Continually worrying about my weight, starving myself was another tantalizing plan. I avoided major food groups like carbohydrates and fats, becoming insecure and irritable as I ignored my hunger pangs. This then developed into an overwhelming, unmanageable wild hunger, and I resembled a saber-toothed tiger that hadn't eaten for months. Every bone in my body was screaming for food. I had to eat, and there was no way to stop it. Unbeknown to me, by restricting myself of food, I was 18 times more likely to develop an eating disorder.

If I weren't starving myself, then I would be bingeing and purging; it became a habit. This overwhelming need to binge, to gain that "high" afterward, of course, kept me from addressing my darn feelings.

So, the slippery path developed. It was as if a devil had taken over my entire thoughts and feelings. I had no control; I was completely powerless around food. Incredibly scared, I didn't know what was happening to me.

Unbeknown to me, statistics now show that one in twenty people with an eating disorder die as a result of their illness.

When I was nineteen, I went to live in Chicago, working as a nanny for my incredibly inspiring, wonderful family: Abby, a pediatrician, who now has grown into a sister figure in my life, and her husband

Steve, who became a father figure, both always positive and there to support and protect me. Steve was also the most incredibly entertaining genius. Hannah, their daughter, was two and a little treasure. Four years later, along came a mini Steve, with the prebirth name of "Pierpoint Elizabeth" before he was born. Luckily, after birth, the fine name of Gerrit was chosen.

With the bulimia implanted in my core, I couldn't control myself. It became a way of life. I remember thinking *'If only I could stop eating completely, then the whole problem would disappear'*. Not quite the right solution, I had to survive. So, if I weren't bingeing and purging, the odd morsel of cheese popcorn kept me going.

Expressing my feelings wasn't on my radar. I didn't know how to verbalize my emotions, something I had never learned, and the bulimia became so detrimental; I would vomit limitless times per day. I had no control over this behavior, as it took over my life, even though part of me felt I was in control. Bingeing and purging was a way for me to release tension and a multitude of enormous, painful feelings.

As I look back at the photos of me in my 20s, I resembled a skeleton, and it wasn't even Halloween. I was thinner than a rake with a huge bloated face. At the time, I wasn't aware of how strange I looked.

I understand now the bloating is caused by the enlargement of the salivary glands, which often occurs in the cheeks and under the jaw, resulting in the characteristic "moon face."

Family and friends were aware but didn't know at that time what to do or say. My mother would come to Chicago periodically and try to talk to me about my bulimia. I was in total denial. In the 1980s, there wasn't much information on eating disorders, let alone specifically bulimia. My denial reminds me of that old phrase, "Keep your head buried in the sand." But not just my head, my whole body, down to my feet, was buried so deep in the sand, you could only see the tips of my toes.

While living in Chicago, I made many amazing friends who, to this day, haven't managed to escape from my grasp. I'm sure they try, but I always manage to hook them back in with my English nonsense.

One day, a great friend said to me, "You're the only person I know who never talks about how you feel." I didn't understand what on earth she meant. I was in complete denial.

We would often venture out to parties. Even if we weren't invited, we would invite ourselves! So, I was well aware of the drug-infused party scene. There was always one bedroom at a party that was full of the usual crowd. With their rolled-up dollar bills tucked behind their ear, ready to snort anything or anyone that came close.

Evidence suggests that people with binge eating and purging disorders are at a much higher risk of illicit drug use and for many, drug use becomes a way to avoid their negative bulimic patterns temporarily. So, stay away from any sort of drug. It's not going to help you whatsoever.

Luckily for me, this wasn't something that worked for me. I had my way of dealing with life, squashing down those feelings until I learned there were far more beneficial ways of dealing with these wretched feelings later in life.

I was so confused about what was going on with my behavior. I repeatedly had one thought whirling around in my brain: 'I am just going mad'. It was the only explanation I could conclude. I had always been on the loopy side, but this was a little extreme!

I was disgusted with myself and my behavior; I felt like I was a failure and not good enough. It would often come back to my limiting belief that I wasn't intelligent enough, especially to figure out how to break free of this madness.

I felt I was broken and the devil had taken over me. But I continued to pretend that I was happy just in case anyone were to find out about the real me and my hidden devil secret. However, most people knew; I was still in total denial.

I now know that I wasn't broken and the devil hadn't taken over me. It was all the side effects of malnutrition, prolonged restriction of food, and, of course, those goddam feelings.

CHAPTER THREE

After an incredible five years of life experiences traveling around the States, weighed down with anorexia and bulimia, I moved back to London. I could no longer live without my loving mother. I had to be closer.

I ended up living with her and my stepfather in Oxford for the first few months. Unquestionably, she could see the secrecy and denial of my secret self-harming. One evening after dinner, as I shamefully hurried from the toilet, she decided again to attempt to speak to me about my bulimia. I remember screaming to myself, *The audacity of it. Not me! What on earth was she talking about?* But eventually agreeing with her, I promised I would try to stop making myself sick and eat like a normal person whatever that was because I had no idea!

As if it were as easy as that!

I then moved to London to a flatshare in Battersea. I had a room just big enough to swing a concussed hairy rat. I got a job working at a large florist as a sales rep. I would survive on one small packet of Walkers salt and vinegar crisps per day. They were delicious, but hardly filling!

I often had a day off during the week. With hardly any friends and all my flatmates, whom I didn't know or like, at work, I would hurry down to the shops, buy as many carbohydrates as I could carry, then stagger back to the flat and have a bingeing feast. Of course, I would then purge multiple times.

After six months, I moved in with my brother in North London, who was away traveling for months at a time. With nothing much else in my life, after a day's work, knowing I would be going home to an empty, lonely flat, physically exhausted with only a meager packet of crisps to keep me energized, I was forever hungry.

My concentration was a struggle, as I was consumed with thoughts of food all day and my stomach permanently ached from the purging. When I got home, I was like a ravenous giraffe with my neck cramming into the depths of the kitchen cupboards to scrabble around for foods to engulf. The only way I knew how to make me feel better, give me a life or a high, was to binge and purge. Of course, the high was a brief, fleeting moment, but it was better than not having any sort of reprieve.

My body ached. I was continuously cold and often resembled an Eskimo. I usually would have dizzy spells, ringing in the ears, and tingling in my fingers and toes that sometimes would go numb. Then, more often than not, I couldn't sleep.

Horrified one day, I found my luscious long blonde hair filling my brush. As the years went on, my hair became thinner, and my skin resembled a dry scaly lizard. I realized that If I continued living like this and didn't get some help soon, I would end up looking like a hobo.

Could it be that my mother and everyone around me were right? I needed to get some sort of help. But how could I survive and eat anything without making myself sick? The anxiety and nervousness would overwhelm me, and I could see no way out. I became impatient and moody with my friends and family and began to withdraw. I became depressed as the walls were closing in.

At age 27, I had been in denial for so many years. One night, my mother came to stay. She broached the subject of my bulimia yet again. She was very calm in tolerating my negative responses. But after a long discussion about my patterns of eating, confronted yet again by her, I felt tremendous anger. I was terrified, and the fear of change was powerful. *Could I ever move on from this?* I thought.

I was and always had been a people pleaser. I felt guilty if I were to think of myself, let alone please myself. I was a professional at pleasing *everyone else*. Maybe it was time to please my mother, so I finally agreed for her to sweep me off to see my doctor.

So, on a blustery autumn morning, I began that long, steep and muddy, slippery road in gaining help. With my lack of insight into the seriousness of my illness, my mother dragged me to the doctor.

I remember the doctor questioning me about the bingeing, and sternly asking, "Why do you make yourself sick?" Well, if I consciously knew the answer, I would stop! I didn't understand why he would ask me such a ridiculous question. But to a rational thinking mind, it was a reasonable question. But here I was buried beneath all the answers struggling to breathe. I had no clue.

I was then sent to Colney Hatch Lunatic Asylum in North London to see a psychiatrist, which was what it said on the sign. It was, as you would imagine, a mental asylum, absolutely petrifying.

The asylum was in operation from 1851 to 1993. It was a typical Georgian building with arches and spires and plenty of wire fences, the building stretching for a mile in length, as mentally disturbed inpatients wandered aimlessly in the corridors and on the grounds.

I had never been to such an institute. I was alone, frightened, and shocked, thinking this was where I was headed, wandering aimlessly for the rest of my life. I scurried along the pathways to the main building. Once inside, scampered along the creepy interminable cobwebbed corridors toward my fate.

I could hear muttering behind me. As I glimpsed back to see a man wearing a shady looking raincoat with only one arm in and the other arm under the coat holding something. He had ankle-length black trousers, a rumpled white shirt, and braces, with a black and white polka dot bowtie.

I quickened my pace and with a fleeting glance over my shoulder, I became aware of the man's bristled eyebrows leading into dark, lanky hair. My mind began racing as I slowed to avoid a woman who had abruptly halted in her tracks in front of me. Wildly, she began to screech the English national anthem.

Suddenly, I felt a tight grasp on my arm, tugging me to a halt. I turned to find it was bowtie man. I became aware of panic beginning to rise from within me. The dark eyebrows slowly came creeping toward mine. With warm, putrid breath, he whispered, "Do you want to play Frisbee?"

In shock, panic flooding my body, I fell backward. Tumbling against the tiled walls, I splattered onto the floor. Finally, managing to splutter, "Sorry, NO," I crawled to my feet and flew from the scene. Glancing back, luckily, he had disappeared.

As I weaved along the dingy corridors, I found the psychiatrist's office and fell into the waiting room. Almost hysterical and overwhelmed with panic. There, standing in front of me was the man with the bristled eyebrows, Frisbeeless, in a crisp, glistening white doctor's coat clutching a stethoscope discussing the weather with the secretary as he scuttled into his office.

The secretary, realizing my angst, kindly took my details, and with many a calming word, asked me to take a seat.

As I awaited my fate, anxiety bubbled that the doctor would confirm I was insane. I thought that going to see a psychiatrist meant that I had indeed lost all my marbles and I was like the other troubled inpatients.

Finally, eyebrows sprung around the corner of his open door as my name was quietly croaked. With my heart bulging from my chest, I tiptoed in. I perched on the edge of my seat, distracted by the two brillo pad eyebrows straining for my attention as they glistened. I proceeded to answer 379 questions. Eventually, eyebrows explained to my surprise that I wasn't going completely bonkers or insane. I, indeed, had bulimia and anorexia. Relief and confusion flowed as he referred me for weekly appointments with their counselor.

Nervously, I built up enough courage to question him about how he managed to race to his office and refresh before me? As confusion matted the eyebrows, suddenly, a glimmer of a smile spread across his face as he proceeded to explain he had a mentally ill twin brother staying at the institution, and this is whom I must have encountered. After that explanation, all I could think about was the fact that there were actually four of these incredible eyebrows in the world.

Eyebrows aside, I did have one problem. I would have to return each week to this eyebrow infested, godforsaken institution. I wasn't sure which was worse—having to see the counselor and begin to learn about myself or returning to this asylum.

I came away even more distraught than when I arrived. How could I ever return to such a bloodcurdling place? After explaining to my brother, Rich, my distressing experience and hearing the panic in my soul, he agreed to take time off work to support me each week. There are no words I can think of to describe what a huge relief I felt hearing him utter such an offer. Having a friend or family member there for support is such an incredible guiding comfort.

So off to the asylum, we would trudge each week, dodging frisbees and ducking and diving wild eyebrows until I became brave enough to venture on my own.

The counselor seemed pleasant enough. She had a couple of long hairs growing from bulbous moles protruding from her chin. Such a distraction I found challenging.

Visiting this institution weekly was a traumatic experience. After a couple of months, I decided this wasn't working for me. I had to do something different.

I eventually found a moleless private counselor whom I saw weekly for six months and who I felt somewhat understood me. Although she was petite with raccoon features, she had overcome an eating disorder herself.

My mind had become so distorted. Once, I watched as she munched on a crumpet. *How could she stay at a healthy weight and eat things like crumpets!* I thought.

Gradually, I learned how my feelings were connected to the function of my bulimia and anorexia. I could start to see a minuscule speck of light at the end of that dark, damp, scary tunnel.

The summer had arrived, and I was feeling slightly positive as the top layer of my feelings connected to food had begun to unfold with the small steps I had taken. Even though the sharp claws of bingeing and purging were still embedded within me, I was starting to make a breakthrough. The bingeing and purging had slightly reduced.

I had a road trip organized with a friend in Chicago for three weeks. Hiring a Lincoln Continental, we then drove down to New Mexico. We were staying with my friend's Aunt and her 20-year-old son, who decided to invite himself with us as we continued our trip to San Diego. We ended up staying with her cousin's male friends. Who seemed friendly enough. Arriving exhausted, we all decided to go out for dinner. Of course, I wasn't hungry; I had eaten a tortilla chip earlier. The friends took us to their favorite bar. I remember standing and talking with one of the chaps. After this, I recall nothing until I woke up to screaming coming from my friend in the single bed next to mine. Lying on top of me was her cousin's friend. He was raping me! Of course, I was hysterical as we both screamed, accusing him of this act. He totally denied it as he pulled up his trousers!

I was shaken to my core, lost in San Diego with limited money, panicking about how to escape. After a hysterical call to my saviors, Abby and Steve in Chicago, they organized our flights to San Francisco, where Steve flew in, met us, and brought us home to Chicago. After the shock subsided, this traumatic experience left me feeling dirty, ashamed, and guilty.

I blamed myself. How could I not see the warning signs? Yes, I had been drinking alcohol, but was it my fault? Two drinks the whole evening, for me, isn't going to cause a blackout. I believe my drink had been spiked. I didn't ask for it or deserve what happened to me. The only person responsible for my assault was the perpetrator, regardless of the circumstances. He raped me!

I returned to life back in London, where I had continual flashbacks, intrusive memories, and nightmares. Oh yes, this sent me spiraling back down into the depths of my full-on bulimic ways.

The guilt was overwhelming; I felt disgusting now not only with being a bulimic but also with the rape. I was a tangled disaster.

CHAPTER FOUR

Before my trip, I had decided the counselor was no longer helping me, so I had terminated therapy. I was feeling like I was being buried alive by my bulimia. I finally found a UK-based charity called the Eating Disorders Association.

Their program looked hopeful. The structure included a weekly telephone call with a specific eating disorder counselor. Via the post arrived a recommended plan of daily foods, which was such a revelation for me. It explained the correct food groups and the amount of food I should be eating daily. Included also was a food and feelings diary for me to complete weekly. Then I would post back in time for our call the following week for the therapist to determine my nutritional progress and how I was doing emotionally when certain behaviors occurred.

As I studied the program and the amounts of food I was meant to eat, I felt overwhelmed. At that time, even one piece of toast for breakfast was too much to manage. But I had made the decision. Now was the time for me to finally take control of the food rather than it controlling me. I had to start somewhere.

This is what I remember of the daily foods that I had to eat:

Breakfast: Two slices of toast or a bowl of cereal.

Snack: A piece of fruit.

Lunch: Two slices of bread/sandwich with meat fillings etc. A yogurt.

Snack: Piece of fruit.

Dinner: A baked potato with tuna salad. Or grilled chicken with rice and vegetables. A dessert.

As my distorted eyes viewed the dinner examples, I wasn't sure about me eating a dessert!

These examples were huge mountains. I never believed I would ever be able to eat half of what was on their list. Let alone everything.

The diary was interesting as it had a column for thoughts and feelings throughout the day. Wow, did I struggle with this column; what feelings? Buried again under cement is where I would find mine. Emotionally tricky to dig out.

I finally began to eat small amounts; I was eating! I would slip up regularly when those darn thoughts and feelings got the better of me, bingeing and purging, but not to the extent I had previously.

Once I began monitoring my eating each week, by phone, the therapist and I would look at the week and begin to try to identify any patterns in my eating. We discussed barriers to change as we created a plan of action and, of course, my negative thoughts and feelings about food, my self-esteem, habits, triggers, urges, and everything else!

As I started to regain control of my eating in specific patterns, the counselor taught me helpful techniques and methods for when my thoughts and feelings had gotten the better of me.

I began to understand that my eating disorder was a brain wiring problem. It would start to rewire if I stopped obeying these urges to binge. But how to do this was the question?

It was an incredible understanding for me as I began to learn how to eat food again. After years of only binge and purging with no idea how to eat, this was revolutionary to me.

Wahoo! Spending three months in this program, I was making progress.

I'm not saying I was free from bingeing and purging once I finished this program. I still had a long way to go and a lot to learn about myself. Plus, I hadn't addressed all my past issues! But it was a positive step forward.

I started dating a wonderful Italian chap. We tied the knot 18 months later.

He knew about my bulimia and was extraordinarily supportive. Being Italian, mealtimes were a big feast, which was a challenge for me. But it helped me with beginning to enjoy food and mealtimes.

At this time, we had three cats, my bingeing and purging patterns were still reducing, and I had a kind, caring husband.

All was going reasonably well until I got a call from my mother. My entertaining, kind, loving, 96-year-old Irish grandmother had passed away. Losing my only grandparent, the shock overwhelmed me. I couldn't accept such a loss. How could she be gone forever? The pain I felt was incredibly powerful. I was devastated. It was the first family member, other than my father, whom I didn't remember, to die.

I managed to hold life together, only having the odd slip-up.

Not long after her incredibly emotional funeral, on my 30th birthday, with grand plans for the occasion, my husband received the news, his father was critically ill with cancer. He caught the first flight home to Italy only to hear his loving father had passed away before his arrival.

The whole experience was traumatic enough. But I managed to continue eating healthily with the devil of my bingeing and purging rising to the surface spasmodically.

Six months later. My mother was the bearer of further struggles. My Aunt and Godmother, who had been a massive love in my life growing up, was in the hospital. Jumping into my car, speedily driving, I made it to her bedside, where she died a few hours later. My grief was immense, and the bingeing and purging had begun to raise its ugly head more frequently. At this point in my life, I wasn't seeing a therapist, but the feelings were building.

A month later, my incredibly witty, kind, caring uncle became ill. Never having a father, he was a massive part of my childhood. He and my aunt would visit weekly and spent much time with us, guiding us through many difficulties in life. I lived with him and my aunt a couple of times when younger residing in London. We spent many hours laughing as he had the most excellent sense of humor. We lost him a few weeks later. I was devastated; all the grief was becoming too much, and the bingeing and purging continued to increase.

The final straw, our loving cat Cecil died!

I could take no more as I became buried beneath the immense grief. I couldn't breathe. It sent me sliding down into the depths of despair. How do I deal with this mountain of feelings? Oh yes, I know how… Thus, the cycle of bingeing and purging began again.

I felt like I was back to square one. My confidence in my ability to overcome this disease had been trodden down below the earth's surface. I was a complete failure, never going to break free permanently and live like a normal person, whatever that may be! I was fearful that I would always have these setbacks; everything felt impossible.

One-third of women overcoming bulimia and anorexia have slip-ups. But this doesn't mean you can't jump on that wagon again and have that horse gallop to freedom, which is precisely what I did eventually.

Loaded with my knowledge of all had learned about myself and my eating behaviors previously, with the support of family and friends, I managed to steer myself and the horse back on the straight unsteady path, cautiously avoiding the rocky, dangerous cliff down into the bottomless depths of bulimia.

My loving mother was always there to help and guide me through the difficult times. Speaking to her daily, she was a tremendous support. After a few months there, I was back on the horse, agreeably clip-clopping along, learning my way to freedom.

At this time, a friend of mine with whom I was working was also taking steps to overcome bulimia and introduced me to her psychotherapist and hypnotherapist, Frances.

This was where the genuine help and guidance came to fruition. Frances was the most incredibly patient, empathetic, unique person.

Frances had walked a similar path, experiencing bulimia, and this knowledge alone was beneficial. She had a personal understanding of the guilt and shame that I felt as well as how disconnected I felt from the rest of the world that didn't honestly know how I was feeling. But she did. Of course, I still hadn't learned how to open up and talk about my emotions.

She saw how fragile I was and taught me how to deal with the multitude of feelings I had buried so deep and avoided for so long. She was a true inspiration, with her insight and great positive motivation, and a perfect example that recovery is wholly feasible and sustainable.

I would visit her weekly. During this time, I found out my mother had myeloma, which is a cancer of the marrowbone. The news felt like a lightning bolt to my heart. But I had to stay healthy to support my mother. I was hysterical and had slip-ups, but with Frances's help, I managed not to totter near that cliff edge. My horse managed to stay somewhat on the straight road.

Her life expectancy was five years, which was too impossible for me to comprehend. I couldn't imagine life without her. So, I never believed that. Of course, she was going to live forever!

I was doing so well with my eating patterns and behaviors and finally starting to shake off all the dirt from my deeply buried feelings. The desire to begin a family increased my focus on eating healthily toward my recovery.

By the time my first son was born, she had had cancer for two years and many rounds of chemotherapy but was progressing remarkably well. On the big day of his arrival, with the painful, traumatic experience behind me, Mother drove from Oxford to Queen Charlotte's hospital in London to finally meet her first grandson. In her excitement, she had tripped over a ramp and broken her leg. I remember seeing her hobble through the door, and I burst into tears, not because she was limping but because, after everything she had been through over the last two years, she was still alive to meet her first grandson. The emotions were exploding.

Spending several days in the hospital, finally, we were discharged, and Mother with her broken leg came to look after baby Luca and me for a week.

As a first-time mother, I had no idea what I was doing, but having my mother beside me was a godsend. Soaking up her affection, experience, and wisdom, I fumbled my way through. She was my nurturing guiding light. What treasured memories I often share with my now 26-year-old Luca.

Four months later, my mother had completed a ten-day successful cancer treatment program; her discharge was imminent. Baby Luca and I had spent a couple of days in Oxford, visiting her hospital bed-side frequently. On this chilly January morning, briefly popping into the hospital to say my farewells before heading back to London, we excitedly made plans for her departure.

The nurse arrived with many cards with ferret tails hanging from them. With confusion, I asked, "What on earth is happening here?" My mind was running wild. Could they be particular chemo fluffy ferret tail earrings? No! It was time to choose the style and shade of her new wig since hair loss was imminent with this round of chemotherapy.

As you would imagine, it was an emotional conversation. At one point, her eyes grew sad, and she whispered, "I'm scared to die." As a wave of terror flooded my body, I gripped her hand and stammered, "That's not going to happen; you've completed the chemo and are escaping today."

With a look of confirmation, she pulled herself up in the bed, took a deep breath, and declared I was right as she drifted back into her self-determination.

After many hugs, we left. Two days later, she was dead. That was my very last conversation with my mother.

My combined mother and father figure ripped from my heart. Everything was colorless and bleak. I was a mess with my world shattered and a baby to look after.

With nature's way of helping me through such an unbearable experience, I slipped into shock. I couldn't feel the pain of her loss.

With half my heart snatched from me as the months passed and trying to function as a mother; eventually, the emotions came flooding in from every direction. The anger, bitterness, resentment, and guilt submerged me. Then along came the already embedded severe loneliness without my adoring mother.

As these escalated, I became depressed and withdrawn. Then, hey, guess what raised its ugly head yet again? Yes, the bingeing and purging cycle began. I had no control over any feelings. I was drowning as the pain consumed me.

I felt I was an absolute failure. My mother would have been so disappointed.

I was already experiencing from my past the colossal unraveling of feelings. Now, with another heavy layer on top of the previously buried feelings, it was a challenge.

I am so thankful that I had my therapist Frances to help and guide me with the enormous, overwhelming emotions. It took me years to come to terms with no longer having my best friend, my mother, by my side.

I spent four years with Frances, and she was a true angel in my life. She taught me how to begin to tune into these negative feelings AND to talk about and express, process, and cope with my emotions in ways that aligned with my life values. Some were so deep and painful, especially after mothers passing. Of course, I didn't want to open these doors and experience these. But slowly, she taught me how to do this.

In the past, I was trying to avoid my emotions in an unconscious effort to try to help myself feel better. What better way than to restrict my food intake, giving me a false sense of control over my life? It gave me comfort and calmed me. It helped me to detach from my feelings and gave me great relief.

After I had binged and purged, I often would feel great sadness, guilt, disgust, along with that lifelong feeling of loneliness.

The old coping strategies I had used for "self-soothing" may have helped me through stressful and traumatic times, but they no longer worked for me.

So, over this period, I began to learn how to express and process my emotions without the constant strain of trying to suppress the beasts. I learned to be able to experience all my feelings, which incorporated both the pleasant and the ugly ones. I was learning to stop allowing my brain to be ruled by thoughts about food and my body.

When my mother passed, I believe that if I hadn't had my weekly therapy with Frances, I wouldn't be here today. She helped me through the most devastating overwhelming grief of losing the shining star in my life plus the traumatic experiences throughout my past.

SO, WHAT EXPERIENCES CONTRIBUTED TO MY BULIMIA?

At this point, when I look back at all these experiences in my life, I believe these specific events contributed to my bulimia:

- The loneliness of being separated from my mother from such a young age. If the separation anxiety had been addressed, maybe I wouldn't have had continually car-ried this cluster of desperate feelings connected to feeling alone right though until I was in my 30s.

- When at boarding school, I would go hungry. Then I expe-rienced the stress of being continually told to always eat everything on my plate, even if I wasn't hungry. And, of course, I had the whole secrecy of hiding my Garibaldi biscuits and other foods. For me, this set a pattern in con-nection with the secrecy of my bulimia. I would do every-thing in my power to try to keep this shocking pattern I had learned and relied on to survive a deep dark secret.

- Again, at boarding school, not knowing how to talk about my sexual abuse experience, I felt unsupported by the adults around me. I didn't have the confidence to do well at school and consequently fell behind with my work. I failed my exams and concluded I must be stupid. I now under-stand that I had developed a limiting belief, which you'll learn about in Step 5. Continually being reinforced over the years, I began to treat the belief as a fact. Although it wasn't a fact, it was based on a lot of evidence! Plus, I had developed other limiting beliefs about myself, such as I was unworthy, a failure, and helpless, which had to be addressed.

- With the multiple family deaths, had I known how to express my emotions, work through my grief, open up and talk about how I felt, the road to recovery would have been far quicker and smoother.

- Because of my intense fear of gaining weight, the thoughts of food would consume me; I would constantly be thinking of when I could next binge. I had no concerns over my weight loss, unlike others around me. All my friends and family knew I had a problem, but I was in complete denial.

FINDING OUT I WASN'T MAD AFTER ALL...

After so many years of difficulties and struggle in life with all the help and incredible guidance I gained from so many phenomenal people, when I finally crawled out the other side, I decided that I needed to help others the same way I had been helped. So, I trained to become a psychotherapist, specializing in eating disorders.

MEMORIES FROM FAMILY AND FRIENDS OF THE YOUNG BULIMIC KATE:

My now, alcohol-free hilarious step-sister, Lulu, had these words to say of her slim memory when my bulimia was bursting from my every pore.

"I remember when I was about 18, and Kate was moving back from Chicago. I was so excited that she would be in the same country as me again. But I noticed she was different, and I couldn't quite put my finger on it. If you didn't know her, you wouldn't have noticed it, but even though she was laughing and smiling, it never quite reached her eyes. I didn't know then what she had experienced, and it was never talked about. Many years later, she opened up to me, and it all made sense! Of course, I was incredibly drunk for most of my teens, all my 20s, 30s and half of my 40s, so I could just be making this up, or was it a dream...."

Theses are emotional words from a fabulous supportive friend when I was in the depths of my bulimia.

"Kate, also known as 'Cakie' (Auntie Cakie, was a name used by my daughter as she couldn't say 'Kate' and it just stuck!). How long have I known her? Well, give or take 35 years.

When we were young, I use to worry about her eating habits - all she ate was junk food such as Doritos, Nachos, cheese popcorn, etc. Never would she sit for a cooked meal. I had strong suspicions of bulimia, but of course, she never shared that with me, or as far as I'm aware, anyone else in our circle of friends at the time.

She would never express her feelings. I tried to call her out once. No messing, a direct question, "why don't you ever share your true feelings?"

But what secrets did she hide? The sad loss of a father she barely knew or remembers. Her beloved mother, who had to cope with three small children. Being sent to boarding school at an early age paid generously by The Masons, but always homesick. When her Mum sadly passed, I was really worried about her. If it wasn't for her firstborn and caring for him, I think she might have done something really stupid.

But everyone loves Cakie (including me, our mutual friends and my other friends in Jersey)   . What's not to love? Kate is a special lady. She is always there for me. I know I can count on her, and that makes her a true friend. The added bonus is she is one of the few people in his world who can truly make me laugh out loud - a gift. Forgot to mention, my husband loves her too.

Her job now is perfect. She gets to listen to other people's problems and does it so well with the intention that "it's good to talk."
Jane Drew.

Touching words from one extremely special and empathetic cousin—Karen

"Growing up, family celebrations were a huge and important part of my childhood. We always had regular annual meetups at Easter and Christmas with my Grandma's sister Aunt Enid, and my Mother's cousins Mike, Richard and Kate. I initially always felt very nervous visiting Chesham as everybody seemed so very grown-up compared to me but Kate always made my sister and I feel at ease chatting about our Christmas gifts and making us laugh! We shared holidays together and I always thought how super cool Kate was, especially when she had a Bay City Rollers cassette one year! Kate is only five years older than me, but as a child seemed so worldy-wise and I was in awe of how unique, gorgeous and outgoing she was—even in her elf boots. I don't think I really had any idea of the turmoil that was bubbling away underneath. I remember family comments about Kate's weight and the word bulimia being mentioned but Aunt Enid was always very tall and slim to me, the boys too, so I thought it was a family gene! When we met in London we would feast at Chiquitos on free tortillas and chili con queso dip a firm favorite with our margaritas! I remember one time at the flat Kate disappearing into the bathroom for a length of time but it was never something we talked about. I am so very lucky we have grown closer as the years have passed through family ups and downs and with the arrival of our amazing offspring, we have shared wonderful times together. Kate is a strong, generous, loyal and independent soul—I am so proud that this book has been written to share her experiences and provide the healing steps to benefit anybody in need." Cousin Karen

Further emotional words from another amazing, empathetic friend reflecting on the young bulimic Kate:

"Kate (or Lady Kate, as we used to call her, with her posh English accent and, as we presumed, then a "privileged" boarding school upbringing) was one of my first friends when I moved to London in 1988. She was this quirkily-dressed, outgoing, confident, and oh-so-skinny young lady! How little I knew the true her then - she hid her pain and bulimia well. Maybe I couldn't see past the fun-loving attitude and the great guacamole she taught me to make! I didn't realize she was surviving on one pathetic packet of crisps a day. Her secret was well hidden.

Fast-forward 30+ years and Kate is still a true friend who has worked on overcoming her traumas to become the wonderful, talented therapist she is today (and frequently makes us both a mean cheese toastie!)" Linda Cottee.

Also, exceptional words from the great Neil Long:

"I believe, personally, the best mentors are people who have experienced the thing they are teaching and are relatable and approachable too. Kate is both of these things. From a deeply harrowing personal story to her own healing process to being a light for others, with powerful techniques for change, she demonstrates that hope and healing is indeed possible."

I love her and love this book! Bulimia Sucks! Let's zap that sucker!

Neil Long, Breakfast Presenter and Podcast coach.
www.neillong.com

TESTIMONIAL

This was a testimonial from a client with bulimia; she was a 25-year-old White English girl and, in a session, once made a comment about how she would really like to be a "strong independent Black woman," which made us both giggle, but this was her goal. I love it.

"Hey Kate,

I'm out in Abu Dhabi again, which is where I was when I first contacted you, and the difference from then to now is absolutely amazing. The things I learned from our sessions helped me more than I ever imagined. Firstly, I'm eating three meals a day (!!!!!!!) with snacks in between. I'm not taking any drugs, and only having the occasional glass of wine. The bulimia is fading away slowly but surely, and only rears its ugly head when I am anxious, which is rare. The thing I hated about myself the most was the way I treated my mum, which was like sh**. Now we laugh and talk nonstop, and I feel real love for her again, and I can't explain how beautiful that feels.

I am still with John, who I feel has been a bloody saint through all this, and I love him more than ever. I am now living happily back in Guildford and loving life.

I just wanted to thank you really because although I know it was your job to help me, I felt like you really cared, and I needed that. I don't think I could have done any of this without you, and I believe you honestly saved my life. So, thank you again and again and again.

All the best
Strong independent Black woman."

RIGHT NOW, WHAT IF YOU DID NOTHING TO CHANGE?

HOW WILL LIFE BE IF YOU DECIDE NOT TO TAKE THAT FIRST STEP?

In the following pages, I'll guide you step by step to begin focusing on making substantial functional changes to your life as you start here and now to break free from your negative habits and behaviors. I want you to imagine what your life would look like if you didn't follow the steps in this book?

 Complete the WHAT IF (YOU DON'T) table in the introduction, in your workbook. Otherwise, grab your notebook and answer these questions:

WHAT IF (YOU DON'T):

	6 MONTHS FROM NOW?	1 YEAR FROM NOW?	5 YEARS FROM NOW?
You don't make that decision to begin to change now. What would be the consequences of that decision on your health?			

What would
be the
consequences
of that decision
on your
your
relationships
with your
loved ones?

What would
be the
consequences
of that decision
on your mind
and body?

If you're like I was, most of the time, you're on autopilot, so the more clearly you can imagine and continue doing what you're doing and how detrimental it will be to your life, the more likely you're to break free from bulimia.

As you picture all the potential negative consequences, it will begin to motivate you to start to make that change. And we want motivation and drive coming from every direction to propel you forward. Throughout this book, you'll be learning practical ways to do this.

HOW WILL LIFE BE IF YOU DECIDE "YES" I AM GOING TO TAKE THAT FIRST STEP?

Okay, you've looked at where you are now if you decide not to begin to change.

So, let's take this forward—you've completed all the steps in this book and begun to cement your pathway to freedom from bulimia. What would life look like?

Your mind, emotions, and body are connected! If your mind can't visualize and see your outcome, then your feelings can't connect with it. So, it's time to use your imagination and visualize how you're going to look, feel, and think in your positive future.

Many of my new clients, when thinking about their future, have a completely blank screen; they can only see their bulimic behaviors ahead of them. If this is how it is for you, then now is the time to learn to visualize your future free from all your debilitating behaviors.

Fill out the table below, being as specific enough that you can see a definite result. This will make it easier for your emotions and mind to begin focusing on how you want to be in the future.

 Complete the WHAT IF (YOU DO) table in the introduction, in your workbook. Otherwise, grab your notebook and answer these questions:

Take a moment to ask yourself:

WHAT IF (YOU DO):

6 MONTHS FROM NOW?   1 YEAR FROM NOW?   5 YEARS FROM NOW?

You have made
that decision to
begin to change
now. What
would be the
consequences
of that decision
on your health?

What would
be the conse-
quences of that
decision on your
relationships?

What would
be the
consequences
of that
decision in your
mind and body?
How good
does this feel?

Great, which is the better option from the two tables? I'm probably guessing the latter, but you might ask, "How do I get there?" Ah-ha! This is what you'll be learning throughout the steps in this book to break through your negative behaviors.

37

In each step, you'll find compelling, incredible exercises to help you move forward and positively change as you learn how to motivate yourself to freedom.

Motivation is inside us all, and it's entirely within your control. With the guidance in this book, you can discover how to unhook it from the muddy, confusing swamp so that it's bubbling inside you right now. Unleash it. Begin to learn the steps of how to spur your intrinsic motivation and watch it flourish while it empowers you to take back control of your life.

"LET TODAY BE THE DAY YOU GIVE UP WHO YOU'VE BEEN FOR WHO YOU CAN BECOME" —HAL ELROD

ARE YOU READY FOR YOUR FIRST STEP?

Allow yourself to take that first step to change. You can do this because moving forward into your recovery, the better prepared you are, the more likely you are to succeed. You need to know what to expect along the way, but the most critical point here's to have a recovery plan.

You, too, can break your chains of bulimia and learn that you are worthy of your life. All your debilitating behaviors can and will change as you work through this book. With all the discoveries, you'll learn about yourself. You can move forward to live that "normal" life everyone else seems to have.

So, whether you're ready or not, jump in; what have you got to lose? Now is the time to take those first leaps toward Step 1 and your new bulimia-free life.

The strength and motivation within you will begin to glow, and as you progress through the steps, it will shine brighter and lighter until it will be so bright, you'll have to install a dimmer switch to control it!

LADY GAGA

This is what Lady Gaga, American singer and actress, says about overcoming bulimia and anorexia:

"I'm proud of my body, and you should be proud of yours too...No matter who you are or what you do. I could give you a million reasons why you don't need to cater to anyone or anything to succeed. Be you, and be relentlessly you" (Eating Recovery Center, 2017).

**"YOU CAN'T START THE NEXT CHAPTER OF YOUR LIFE
IF YOU KEEP RE-READING THE LAST ONE"**

ARE YOUR READY? YEAHHHHHH... COME ON... HERE WE GO... ITS TIME TO STEP INTO YOUR NEW FUTURE...AND LET YOUR SECRETS UNRAVEL AS YOU REPROGRAM YOUR DAZZLE...

STEP 1 THIS WAY...

STEP 1

WHY DO I MAKE MYSELF SICK?

"WHAT YOU DID IN THE PAST REPRESENTS WHO YOU WERE THEN. WHAT YOU DO NOW REPRESENTS WHO YOU'RE BECOMING"

It all began with one breath. A simple sentence! As easy at that.

Growing up, I was always a skinny little rake, without the spikes. As a teenager, I started to fill out slightly, and some would say, "developing into a shapely woman!" But it was a stark, dark change for me.

One fateful day, I invited a friend over for dinner. We finished our exceptional cuisine delight and, as girls do, we discussed our weight, calories, food, and everything to do with our non-existent weight issues.

Suddenly, her voice rose excitedly. "Did you know if you were to eat a Mars bar, then made yourself sick afterward, you won't put any weight on?" For me, it wasn't just a light bulb moment but a luminous multi-colored neon strip light moment. What an ingenious idea!

I grabbed it with not only both hands but also my feet and ran with it as fast as I could!

Even Princess Diana stated in transcripts of tapes published by *The Daily Mail*, "The bulimia started the week after we got engaged [and would take nearly a decade to overcome]. My husband [Prince Charles] put his hand on my waistline and said: 'Oh, a bit chubby here, aren't we?' and that triggered off something in me."

Oh, how powerful one suggestion can be!

In this first step on your pathway to freedom from bulimia, you'll be:

- Learning the causes of why you're bingeing and making yourself sick.
- Understanding what your functions or "needs" of your life-threatening destructive behavior are.
- Understand how you can transform your focus and begin to visualize how you want to be in your future to freedom.
- Also, discover how you can start to reprogram your incredible mind to transform your negative thinking to positive, powerful motivational thoughts and feelings.

As you work through this book, rather than flying through each step, I want you to make deliberate, specific slow steps and learn how you're going to completely break all the chains linked to why you have bulimia.

There's a lot to learn, so let's begin...

SO WHY DO I MAKE MYSELF SICK?

When I had bulimia, this was a question that baffled me. Why on earth would I make myself sick? I must be crazy. I was so confused and didn't believe that I could stop this pattern.

But let me tell you here and now, YOU **CAN** *STOP* YOUR BINGEING AND MAKING YOURSELF SICK; it's true. I haven't binged or made myself sick for 25 years, and with the right tools, you too **can change now**.

If only recovery were that simple!

There are multiple reasons why you've ended up down this dark, scary path, and you're now going to begin to learn what has kept you hooked into this destructive behavior.

As you deprive yourself of food, the bingeing and purging cycle begins, the causes and the multitude of feelings connected to these causes are put on hold. As you binge and purge, providing some sort of fleeting pleasure and instant relief or release, no longer feeling guilty for having the food in the stomach, some say they're on a high and feel relaxed. Unfortunately, this is only temporary because then the guilt, secrecy, and physical side-effects begin to build up again. The exhausting painful patterns begin all over again. It's like being on a roundabout that's spinning so fast; you can't see a way off and round and round you go.

If it were that simple just to stop bingeing and purging, then you would have done this already! But, usually, many factors in a person's life are preventing them from stopping now.

ITS TIME TO RIP OFF THAT BAND-AID AND ADDRESS
WHAT IS ACTUALLY GOING ON FOR YOU

SO, WHAT ARE THE REASONS PEOPLE GET BULIMIA?

You may have an idea of why you have bulimia, or maybe you don't. My brain was one complete muddle of confusion as to why I was engulfed in this uncontrollable behavior. Having a clearer understanding of how you've gotten there will be so incredibly powerful in helping you to clearly see how you're going to break all your negative habits and patterns.

Let's begin by looking at the reasons why people develop bulimia.

1. ABUSE AND BULIMIA

Most people with bulimia have been preoccupied with dieting and food for many years. Their binge and purging behavior may be triggered by trauma from abuse. From multiple studies taken, there's a higher possibility that if you've been sexually abused when young that you'll develop bulimia. And with that comes colossal feelings of shame, guilt, and need for a way to numb the emotions connected to that memory. It could be a way to punish themselves, or it could be a kind of comfort or protection, for when someone has been sexually abused, the world can then feel unsafe.

When people are sexually abused, their boundaries of themselves have been violated, which can have a detrimental effect on their eating habits and body image. This also can have such an immense impact that it can become challenging to recognize feelings of hunger, tiredness, or sexuality.

So, turning to food is a way to cope with their feelings and to release a multitude of negative emotions that actually have nothing to do with real hunger. The bubbling confusion and uncertainty about themselves brings their focus to food.

You may feel a loss of control over your safety. With bulimia, this pattern of behavior will be providing relief from distressing feelings, unconsciously regaining feelings of control and safety. Your intention isn't the pain but the good emotions or pleasure that you get from this. You're looking for ways to relieve the pain by bingeing and purging to get that "high" or pleasure afterward.

As you read in the memoir, I was sexually abused when I was young. The multitude of feelings I had in connection with the abuse was buried so deep within me, and this pattern continued for 25 years until I was ready to face it, talk about it, work through all the beastly feelings, and then let them go.

NEGATIVE BODY IMAGE

What is body image?

Body image is identified as your thoughts, opinions, and attitude about how you look. It's sadly not uncommon to dislike your appearance, and people who develop bulimia are more likely to report higher levels of body image dissatisfaction.

A negative body image is a distorted view of your shape. Plus, along with this comes all those self-destructive feelings of self-consciousness, shame, and anxiety.

A positive body image is a realistic view of how your body looks. Feeling comfortable and confident about what you see, accepting your natural body size and shape.

"MIRROR MIRROR ON THE WALL, ITS TIME TO CHANGE YOUR VISION ONCE AND FOR ALL"

BODY DYSMORPHIA

What is body dysmorphia?

Body dysmorphia, also known as imagined ugliness, in which your imagination, as powerful as it is, goes wild and becomes extremely confused with how you look. You could have a minor flaw, say a pimple, that you embellish into an ugly beast, then scratch it to increase the ugliness.

Body dysmorphia can also include:

- Continually asking for reassurance on your looks
- Changing your clothes constantly
- Becoming obsessed with grooming yourself

It can become so extreme and distressing with the flow of never-ending feelings of shamefulness that you may not want to be seen by anyone.

Many people have areas of their body they aren't happy with. But research shows that approximately 80% of people with body dysmorphia report they have experienced suicidal thoughts, which is 10 to 25 times more intense than the general population.

BODY DYSMORPHIA AND BULIMIA

Many people with bulimia suffer from body dysmorphia symptoms. Usually, the focus is on the body weight or the shape and checking their body for any flaws, intensifying the negative feelings and thoughts you may have about your weight and shape.

I remember when I was in the depths of bulimia, every time I looked in the mirror, all I could see was a bulbous fat lump! This wasn't true; I was skinny and totally distorted what was in that mirror. So, for your recovery, it's essential that you now stop looking in any mirror. They're doing you so much harm and will hinder your fantastic vision of recovery.

> **"OUR MINDS DISTORT WHAT WE SEE IN OUR MIRRORS, LIKE WORDS DISTORT THEIR MEANING" —ADITI GAUR**

LOW SELF-ESTEEM

What is low self-esteem?

Having bulimia is terrible enough, but along with this comes low self-esteem, which is struggling with:

- Feelings of Inadequacy
- Looking at faults in your character
- Feeling incompetent in some way
- Feeling unlovable

Low self-esteem causes you to think and feel as if you aren't good enough in how you look, how you perform at school or work, and how you relate with friends and family. It's as if your life had no value and purpose.

Do you think you have low self-esteem?

If you do, it will take time to change; these negative thoughts and feelings may have been there for a long time.

Although, if you're still starving yourself, your brain and your body will be malnourished, and you'll find it difficult to change your thoughts and feelings connected to low self-esteem rationally.

Working through the steps in this book, you can begin to learn how to value and believe in yourself, and appreciate YOU for the incredibly wonderful, beautiful individual you are.

WESTERN CULTURE AND THE UNREALISTIC

Oh yes, you're surrounded by stunning slim models with the ideal body everywhere you look, in magazines, posters, TV, and social media.

You're influenced to think that these women are of average weight and body shape, and this is where we get the belief that being thin is going to make us popular, happy, and successful. But alas, this is an unrealistic view of life. These images become unconsciously seeded into our minds, even though part of us knows that the images are inaccurate.

A study of Fiji islanders is a great example:

In 1995, the island of Fiji had no reported cases of bulimia, anorexia, or weight problems because they had no access to television, which was marvelous. But once the TV was introduced and after three years of watching American and British TV shows, more than two-thirds of Fijian girls had learned how to diet, and three-quarters of them felt "too fat." Such negative learning for these girls is a perfect example of the life we live in.

So much research has shown that this exposure leads us to body dissatisfaction and striving to replicate the unrealistic slim models, which then causes eating disorders, including bulimia.

BULLYING

Many of my clients discuss how they were bullied when younger, particularly as teenagers. With hormones floating where they shouldn't, they can often become extremely conscious of their physical appearance.

Consequently, if they are bullied about their weight, size, shape, or looks, huge painful emotions can sweep in, causing feelings of shame and sadness and leading to further unruly thinking, such as insecurities, low self-esteem, body image, and depression.

Nowadays, with so much social media, teenage discussion, and peer pressure to look a certain way, to fit into what they think others find appropriate, they feel they must take action, and in steps the big B - bulimia.

Being bullied can bring on feelings of being out of control. Developing bulimia gives them a sense of control back, so at least they can control one area of their life, even if it's detrimental.

THE DREADED WORD...DIETING!

Dieting is one of the most influential risk factors for developing bulimia. It affects your brain, influencing mood changes, increasing the preoccupation around food and negativity around body issues. Focusing on dieting can become a great escape to what? Oh, yes, to what you are genuinely thinking and feeling.

If you want to fail... then diet!

Any thoughts of dieting must stop; diets don't work. Some lose weight dieting. But they end up putting all the weight back on and usually with extra rolls of fat also.

That's because they haven't addressed the real reasons why they were reaching out for foods when they weren't hungry. Plus, they haven't explored the unconscious triggers, links, and patterns of their real thoughts and feelings.

STRESSES IN LIFE

Stress is how your body responds to different pressures from a situation. Too much stress can affect your attitude, body, and relationships and can vary from person to person, making you feel anxious or grouchy.

It could be connected to a significant change in your life, such as:

- A change of job
- Move to a new home
- Maybe a relationship issue like rejection from a boyfriend or divorce

- Death of a loved one

Significant changes like these could increase the risk of developing bulimia.

For me, apart from my abuse when younger, I believe one of the reasons I developed bulimia was because at the age of 17, I was released from the strict but relatively stress-free confinements of boarding school. I was then suddenly faced with the stress of coping on my own in the big overwhelming lonely town called London. My mother, remarried, sold our family home and moved to another area.

For more information on stress, see Step 5.

PERFECTIONISM

Are you perfect? I hope not!

Perfectionism is setting unrealistically high expectations for yourself, which is difficult ever to ever achieve because, no matter, it could always be better. And if you haven't achieved this goal, then, here comes your evil voice to beat you up. If you try to be consistently perfect and portray an ideal image, you cannot be genuine; you can't be true to yourself.

Focusing on assignments, work deadlines become overwhelming as you create pressure on yourself to achieve and make perfect. And when this isn't met, the great FoF comes in—Fear of Failure.

If a perfectionist is trying to lose weight to have that "perfect" appearance, whatever that may be—but I don't think it actually exists—the pressure piles up. If they aren't achieving their weight loss goals and put on a pound, then in swarms the huge FoF. The feelings of low self-worth engulf them, which then can lead to:

- Compulsively exercising
- An increase in laxatives or diuretics
- Counting calories
- Bingeing and purging

**"STOP TRYING SO HARD TO FIT IN;
YOU WERE BORN TO STAND OUT"**

FAMILIES

Oh, we love our families, or do we! Unfortunately, we can learn their harmful habits and behaviors. Studies of families have found that if a parent or sibling has an eating disorder, this can increase a person's risk of developing an eating disorder also.

If they're forever discussing their weight, size, and shape or over-exercising, the child will learn this is acceptable behavior and follow likewise.

If they're judgmental about others and their weight, the child will learn then that how they look in their body is a measure of self-worth, and they could worry that they too will be judged or worry about a poor body image.

If they're overprotective and wanting perfection, they'll put pressure on the child, having high expectations for a huge achievement

Then if they can't live up to all that's wanted from them and they can't control all they need to do. The FoF slithers in, and they may look elsewhere for something that they can control, which is dieting. That could lead them to binge and purging. And the whole bulimia cycle begins.

Troubling issues within the family may also be the cause of bulimia; if a person is from a family with many negative behaviors, such as alcoholism, drug addiction, marital fighting, divorce, or domestic violence, these could contribute to bulimia.

Having looked at the causes of your bulimia, let's begin to address what the function of your bulimia is.

WHAT IS THE FUNCTION OF YOUR BULIMIA?

By this, I mean the purpose, need, reward, or reason for behaving the way you do. So, for the sake of simplicity, I call it the function of your bulimia.

Once you begin to understand why your bulimia is serving a function, it becomes much easier for you to know why it's so difficult to stop the patterns of behavior—and how you're going to begin to learn to replace this function positively.

THE FIRST STEP IS AWARENESS OF HOW AND WHY YOU ARE BEHAVING THIS WAY

Let's start to break down your pattern of behavior. I want you to tune into and specifically think about how to identify the possible functions that bingeing and purging serve.

To begin with, look through the list below and see if you identify with any?

It helps me to cope with an enormous amount of negative thoughts and feelings.
It's a way to punish me for reasons, only I may know.
It's an attempt toward perfectionism.
It's my only way to gain comfort in my life.
It's the only way I can have any kind of control in my life.
It's a way to control my weight.
It's a way to distract me from the stress of daily life.
It's my way to shout for "Help."
It's a way to relieve boredom.
It's a way to suppress traumatic memories or feelings of anger or anxiety.
It's a way to gain relief or some sort of freedom.
It's a way for me to rebel against the "Good Girl."

Great! Having read through the list, now make up a list of your personal functions of your bulimia.

 Complete the FUNCTIONS OF YOUR BULIMIA TABLE in Step 1, in your workbook. Then zip back here and continue. Otherwise, grab your notebook and list the functions of your bulimia.

Well done, but you may be surprised that your bulimia isn't about weight loss so much, even though that's a significant concern. So much more is going on that's keeping you clutching to this pattern of behavior.

Thinking about your list and creating your own functions, you can then become:

- More aware of your eating triggers, patterns, and habits.
- More aware of your values and desires.

Now that you've written out your detailed list, here's the exciting part; we need to reevaluate the function causing your bulimia.

Thinking about your list of "functions" now, write down what you could do differently to begin to satisfy these.

 Complete the TIME TO CHANGE TABLE in Step 1, in your workbook. Then zip back here and continue. Otherwise, grab your notebook and list:

YOUR OLD FUNCTION/NEED

WHAT YOU CAN CHANGE/DO DIFFERENTLY

Fantastic, now you have a clearer idea of what your functions are and how you can begin to replace them. We'll be working with those functions throughout the book.

So, let's continue on your exciting new journey of changing the functions of negative thoughts, feelings, and limiting beliefs that have led you down this dark tunnel. Into new positive ways of thinking, feeling and learning about your incredibly powerful mind and how you can begin to use it to change how you think and feel.

"THOUGH NO ONE CAN GO BACK AND MAKE A NEW START, ANYONE CAN START FROM NOW AND MAKE A BRAND-NEW END"—CARL BARD

YOUR MIND IS INCREDIBLY POWERFUL, SO HERE'S WHAT YOU NEED TO KNOW

As an eating disorder therapist, what I've learned over the last twenty-one years is how incredibly powerful your mind is, and this is what I am going to teach you. So you can truly get the help you need to begin to take back control of your life.

Let's learn about your incredible mind. Actually, you have two minds: your conscious mind and your unconscious mind. They both have different functions, so let's look further at the differences between the two.

Your conscious mind?

Your conscious mind is your everyday thinking mind, your logical mind. It constantly whispers in your ear, saying, "You've had such a stressful day. Go ahead and binge and purge; you'll feel better afterward." It consists of 10–12% of your mental capacity.

It's the mind that takes care of physical reality life and is governed by the senses such as sight, hearing, touch, taste, and smell.

Your unconscious mind?

Your unconscious mind is when you're on autopilot. It keeps you breathing regularly, beats your heart for you, and does everything you don't think about to keep you functioning healthily.

Your unconscious mind is always listening and is like the bus driver of your mind.

Your unconscious mind consists of 88–90% of your total mental capacity, which registers everything. You have approximately 60,000 different thoughts every day. Your unconscious mind remembers everything, but your conscious mind doesn't.

Your unconscious mind always tries to help and protect you. It learns lessons quickly from different experiences you may have. For example:

When I was young, consistently being told I was stupid, my unconscious mind learned from this. It then began to help me to think like this and believe that I wasn't smart.

Your habits and thinking

Your unconscious mind stores all your habits of thinking and acting, memorizing all your comfort zones and works on keeping you in this bulimic pattern.

So, all the various techniques I'll be giving you in this book will help reprogram your powerful unconscious mind. You can change your old habits and patterns and focus on how you want to be positive in the future.

Imagine your conscious mind as the garden where
you plant seeds. And your unconscious mind is where
the seeds flourish if nurtured and fertilized.

So rather than planting bindweed, you can begin to plant poppy seeds that will flourish into spectacular huge red poppies.

HAVE YOU EVER STOPPED AND WONDERED HOW YOU THINK?

LET'S LEARN ABOUT SUBMODALATIES

When you think of the specific process of how you do anything, you'll see it has many different factors called submodalities. These are the building blocks of how you think, feel and react to certain things. It's taken from the fantastic therapy called NLP (Neuro Linguist Programming), which is how you can reprogram your unconscious mind to empower yourself to begin to change the way you think and feel.

Learn to master your mind and negative behaviors, including creating a new healthy self-image and shifting your focus into a new healthier you.

NLP is based on the techniques created by Richard Bandler and John Grinder.

It's time to start being aware of how and what you're thinking, what you're saying to yourself that sweeps you into the harmful thinking that then drives you to binge.

Once you begin to notice all those thoughts rattling around in your brain, then you can start to change the way you're thinking.

When we think, there's a pattern to our thoughts, we either:

Think in pictures
Think in words
Think in feelings
Think in tastes or smells

Most people think in both words and pictures; maybe for you, one is more dominant than the other.

 If I were to ask you how you bought this book, did you skip into a book shop and make the purchase there, or did you hop onto (but not literally) your computer or phone to make the purchase?

When you think about that, there will be different elements or steps of how you found your way to the answer...

You would have had:

- An image of you hopping or skipping to the shop to make the purchase.
- A verbalization of where you bought it.
- A feeling about buying it, maybe an exciting feeling?

Let me explain further what submodalities are and how they're going to help you

Your submodalities are the representations of how you view your world. They form the basic building blocks of how you think, feel, and react to certain things; people or events. We'll be working with submodalities throughout the book, so listen up...

Submodalities are made up of five different types; corresponding to the five senses:

Visual Submodalities (Pictures)

It's the picture you have in your mind, which could be:

- A movie or still picture?
- In panorama or a framed picture?
- In color or black and white?
- How bright/dim is the picture?
- Focused or blurred?
- Associated or disassociated?
- What's the size of the picture?
- Close up or far away?
- Are you in the picture or looking at the picture?

Auditory submodalities (Things you hear)

If you hear a sound in your mind, possible characteristics include:

- Words or sounds
- Tone
- Constant or intermittent
- Loud or quiet

- High or low pitch
- Timbre
- Duration
- The direction of the voice
- Tempo

Kinesthetic submodalities (Feelings and sensations)

This is your feelings and sensations; they may include:

- Location - where it is in the body
- Shape
- Quality
- Intensity
- Temperature - Hot or cold
- Texture—rough or smooth
- Pressure
- Constant or intermittent
- Still or moving
- Steady or intermittent
- Direction
- Breathing rate
- Size

Gustatory and Olfactory Submodalities (Taste and Smell)

- Sweet
- Sour
- Aroma—strength
- Bitter
- Fragrance
- How strong is the smell?

Are you still listening up? Because you'll be zipping back to this sub-modalities page often as you work through some of the techniques in this book.

ARE YOU READY TO LEARN HOW YOU CAN FEEL GOOD ANYTIME?
Yessss, here we go...

SO LET'S LEARN ABOUT ANCHORING

 A real key to helping you to take back control of your life is with another NLP (Neuro-Linguistic Programming) technique called anchoring. Anchoring is the connection between a trigger and a change of mood.

Your life has been affected by anchors all your life, even though you haven't created them intentionally. For example: If someone were to smell freshly mowed lawn, that could remind them of when they were young child, a summer day, and Dad had just cut the lawn. Or when you hear a specific song, it reminds you of a past experience or person. These are NLP anchors.

So, whether the anchor is positive or negative and where you are now, you have many problematic anchors that are creating negative responses. Still, the good news is that they work instantly and don't involve rational thinking. You could see, think, or hear about something, and then, automatically, your mood changes, whether you want it to or not. But positive anchors evoke good, pleasant feelings.

Some of the techniques throughout the book will include anchoring, which will be so powerful for you to use when you aren't feeling so positive about yourself.

How you can use anchoring and submodalities positively

You're going to begin by creating a new positive goal of how you want to be in the future. You need the vision to focus on, and, as Tony Robbins says:

"The most important thing that'll drive you is your ability just to sit down and create a vision of how you want to be and each day to live it in your mind. That simple visualization or, if you don't think you make pictures, that simple sense of feeling what you're going to feel like when you've achieved your goals, when you are living in the body that you deserve. That's what'll give you the drive, that's what'll give you the power."

By reinforcing positive self-images with powerful, positive feelings, you start to teach your brain that you want to change to bring you more things that make you feel better, even enjoyable. If you don't believe me, try this out for yourself!

Here we go, your next step to motivate you to begin reprograming your mind to start now to thinking differently and positively:

"THE NEW YOU" TECHNIQUE

Now it's time to use your anchoring and submodalities skills, so here's a simple but incredibly powerful technique that will reprogram your unconscious mind to begin your pathway to freedom.

Read through all the steps, so you know where you're going with this. I don't want you to get lost!

1. First, imagine how you like to be in the future free from bulimia. What would you be doing, thinking, feeling, saying to yourself? Happy, healthy, excited, free.

2. Look at all the details of how you would look; standing upright, feeling confident, smiling, positive, and happy.

3. Now make this image as powerful as possible now to use your new skill of changing the submodalities of your image. Go through your list of submodalities and make this picture as empowering as possible, changing it as follows:

   • Make the colors brighter and bolder.
   • Make the image life-size or bigger, if possible.
   • What would you be saying to yourself? "I'm finally happy and living the life I've always dreamt of."
   • How would you be feeling? Motivated, empowered, excited for your new future.

   Change the movie if you need to, so it's the most empowering movie you've ever watched.

4. Now, step into this incredible new you, so you're actually in the picture, looking through your own eyes, feel what you'll be feeling not to have binged for months or even years. What are you saying to yourself? Something like, "I'm free and so proud of myself." Now intensify the feelings, making them as big and powerful as possible.

5. Now step out of your new image, fantastic, how good did that feel? Brilliant! You can jump right back in there as often as you wish.

You did it! I want you to step into THE NEW YOU every morning and evening. Then periodically through-out each day. Repetition is the key to your achieve-ment. You're reprogramming your unconscious mind, reminding it of the positive direction you want to go in, and it will help you to focus on it.

If you don't *believe me*, try it out. What have you got to lose? It works. You'll start to see a new empowered you. It will help you incredibly to begin to change.

Begin now; it's so exciting to see how you're going to look and feel in this new empowered YOU.

Video Demonstration Link: https://bulimiasucks.com/a-new-you/

"SETTING GOALS IS THE FIRST STEP IN TURNING THE INVISIBLE INTO VISIBLE" —TONY ROBINS

PAULA ABDUL - AMERICAN SINGER

Paula Abdul struggled with bulimia for 15 years, and through therapy, she learned that this was her way of suppressing her feelings. Her weight was linked to her self-worth, and dealing with her difficult emotions helped her recover from bulimia.

She says: "Battling bulimia has been like war on my body. Me and my body have been on two separate sides. We've never, until recently, been on the same side. I felt nervous and out of control, and all I could think about was food. Food numbed the fear and anxiety. I'd eat and then run to the bathroom. I thought, 'God I'm not per-fect. I'm going to disappoint people.' It became a living hell for me. Whether I was sticking my head in the toilet or exercising for hours a day, I was spitting out the food—and the feelings."

STEP 1 - HERE ARE YOUR KEY EMPOWERING ACTION STEPS:

Now is the time you can start to feel proud of yourself for having read through and taken the vital first action steps to begin to slow down your merry-go-round and change the way you're thinking and feeling about yourself and where you are.

- Having read the causes of what has brought you down this destructive path, you may be able to identify with many different areas that have caused you to develop bulimia. But I don't suppose you thought it would become this addictive.
- Now that you have a clearer picture of why you're binge-ing and purging and learning from your own specific list of your unconscious functions behind your behaviors, you'll start to open up to ideas of how you can change positively.
- As you start to acknowledge the importance of beginning to learn to eat like a normal person, your body will reward you in so many positive ways; you won't recognize yourself!
- Practice stepping into "The New You."
  Now you have a new positive picture of how you want to be in the future. Remember, repetition is critical. Each time you jump into this new you, you're reinforcing how you want to be in the future.

Hurrah, you've finished Step 1! I'm so proud of you already. You're opening up to the possibility there's a life without the chains of bulimia.

Are you ready? Do you want some motivation? It's time to flip that page and move on... wahooooo... here we go.

STEP 2

HOW DO I STOP MAKING MYSELF SICK?

"TODAY IS YOUR NEW FUTURE; YESTERDAY IS IN YOUR PAST" —KATE HUDSON–HALL

Your empowering learnings from Step 1:

- In Step 1, you read about what could have caused your destructive behavior. Are there areas that maybe need to be investigated further? If there are, start to think about how you could change this and begin to break your destructive patterns.
- Also, now you have begun to list the reasons and functions that create your chain reaction, leading to your bingeing and purging, or an increase in exercise to help you to cope with life and satisfy your particular needs. What have you done in the beginning to replace those needs? Continue listing new needs when they come up, as, throughout this book, you'll learn techniques to begin to change these patterns.
- Having learned the importance of working with your mind and stepping into "The New You," supercharging the pow-

erful feelings of how you want to be free from all these negative behaviors, repeat it as often as you can.

The positive guidance you'll be learning here in Step 2:

- Arrrharrr, this is where you're going to get that motivation pumping and learn a fantastic technique for whenever you aren't feeling empowered to stay on track with all the incredible changes you've already learned and will be making.
- We'll then move on to investigate the patterns of your draining bulimic cycle. By limiting your food intake and dieting, you cause massive tension and cravings. Along sweeps in your eating triggers, causing your urges to become so overpowering that you end up with your head in the fridge, bingeing on any foods you can find. Then, to free yourself of the guilt, etc., you purge to gain that relief, if only briefly, and then swoops in the feelings of shame, disgust, regret, and self-criticism. We'll be learning how you can begin to make incredibly positive changes to this pattern of events.
- To begin to break down your bulimic cycle, we'll be addressing your triggers to understand what your specific triggers are and then learning an incredible technique to break this pattern.

BUT FIRST... ITS NOW TIME TO MOTIVATE YOURSELF AND TAKE THE NEXT STEP...

What you need now is layers of MOTIVATION, MOTIVATION, MOTIVATION...

How often have you tried to stop your destructive patterns, and maybe it works for a time only to end up giving in and falling back into the cycle? How often have you wished you had the motivation to learn from your slip up and jump back onto a positive path?

How would you like more motivation to help you to take huge leaps toward stopping this bulimic cycle of bingeing a purging?

So, let's learn how you can become motivated instantly...

What I suggest you do anytime you aren't feeling very motivated or confident about taking any of the steps is run through this empowering technique over and over again, to get you fired up and ready to move on to the next step.

We'll be creating connections between feeling wholly motivated and not feeling entirely motivated to stay focused on your path to freedom.

Trust me... it works and is a fantastic tool to have right at your fingertips for whenever you aren't feeling positive about all the incredible changes you're making.

Please read the steps first, so you have a clear picture of what you need to do.

"ELECTRIFY YOUR MOTIVATION" TECHNIQUE

Let's first create a positive, motivated feeling:

PART 1

1. On a scale of 1—10, how strong is your motivation to free yourself of your bulimia, with 1 being similar to a water pistol in strength compared to 10 being the most powerful similar to a fire hose.
2. Okay, so now think of something that you're already motivated to do, like your favorite hobby, spending time with family, going on holiday, or if you won the lottery (how motivated would you be to go and spend the money?)
3. Visualize the movie, seeing it through your own eyes as though it's happening right now, imagine what you would see and hear, and feel exactly how being motivated feels. When you're entirely into how that feels, squeeze together with your thumb and index finger of your left hand.
4. Keep going through that motivational movie. As soon as it finishes, start again, continually squeezing your finger and thumb together while you feel that motivation.
5. Stop. Now test your motivation trigger. Squeeze your thumb and finger together and relive that good feeling. It may not feel as intense, but the more you do this, the more enhanced that feeling will become.

PART 2

Now to make the connection between feeling motivated and your negative behaviors. You're about to become super motivated to changing these patterns.

1. Squeeze your thumb and finger together of your left hand and remember what it's like to feel motivated.

2. Imagine yourself free from bulimia and going throughout the day, enjoying yourself, thinking of what you would do, how great life will be, not thinking about food all the time that leads you to binge and purging or over-exercising or calmly leaving those laxatives in the cupboard.

3. Imagine things going perfectly, exactly the way you want them to. See, feel, and hear how good it feels. Do this again, still squeezing your thumb and finger together of your left hand, permanently associating motivation to taking the positive steps to free yourself.

4. Scale 1 -10 how motivated do you feel to take the steps and start to address the good new positive changes you're going to make? The higher the number, the more comfortable you'll find it to break all your delicate patterns and habits linked with your bulimia. The lower the number, the more you need to practice the technique. (Taken from Paul McKenna's book I Can Make You Thin).

 Great, now keep running through this technique to build on your motivation and then using this when you aren't feeling confident about the changes you're making.

Video Demonstration Link: https://bulimiasucks.com/electrify-your-motivation/

"INSIDE YOU, THERE IS MOTIVATION READY TO FLOURISH"

SO HOW DO I STOP THIS CYCLE OF BINGE EATING AND MAKING MYSELF SICK?

This was the first question I wanted answered when I bought a book on bulimia. I was so low and in such colossal despair and confusion. With all my willpower, I just couldn't stop the horrific pattern of bingeing and purging.

I had no control, but then this was the only thing in my life I could control, none of it made any sense to me, and it took me years to find the right support. But with all the areas you're going to be addressing as you work through this book, you instantly have the answers right here at your fingertips.

HOW AM I GOING TO MAKE THIS CHANGE?

This could well be one of the main reasons why you bought this book, hoping there's a magic wand inside the book, and with one quick wave, you'll have the answer to how you can stop making yourself sick.

Well, unfortunately, there's no magic wand inside the book but something even more magical...

MOTIVATION, LEARNING, TOOLS, AND TECHNIQUES to help you to stop this dreaded pattern of bingeing and purging once and for all.

BUT FIRST, you need to begin to understand your habits, patterns, and triggers so you can start to break this bulimic cycle and eventually to feel happier in your life.

'Happier' what a fine word! That may not seem very close to you right now, but it may be closer than you think once you've read and followed this program because you can change once you have the tools.

THE BULIMIC MERRY-GO-ROUND

The bulimic cycle is just like being on a merry-go-round and round and round you go. Something triggers your agonizing urges, which sends you to overeat and then vomit. You suddenly feel briefly relieved, but then the overwhelming thoughts and feelings of guilt and self-criticism begin again.

So rather than slowing down your merry-go-round so you can hop off, it often speeds up and spins so fast, you'll be lucky to retain your case, let alone your phone, as you fly off into the abyss! Let's look at the pattern of the bulimic cycle:

YOUR BULIMIC CYCLE

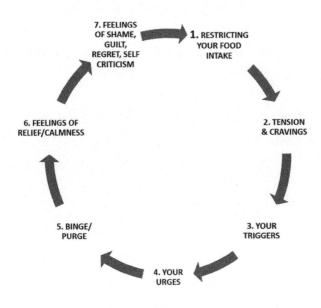

One of the main reasons you binge is to remove your uncomfortable "urges to binge." If you could learn to be more accepting of your binge urges, they wouldn't cause you so much difficulty, and then you would be in a better position to ignore them rather than act on them.

HOW FAST IS YOUR ROUND ABOUT SPINNING?

Let's talk about where you are now, and your binge-purge cycle of behavior, otherwise known as the chain of events.

What are the chains of events that cause this pattern to spin?

1. Limiting your food intake by dieting.
2. Which causes massive tension and cravings.
3. Then up spring your vulnerable eating triggers. You see, feel, hear, taste, or smell something that triggers you.
4. Your urge to eat builds into uncontrollable fear and panic.
5. Which then automatically sends you into the fridge where you eat as much as you can then purge.
6. Then the relief and feelings of calmness floods in briefly.
7. The final link in the chain of events is the feelings of shame, guilt, disgust, self-criticism, regret, etc.

It feels like this chain is on a never-ending cycle repeating itself as it becomes a habit.

LET'S TAKE A CLOSER LOOK AT YOUR CHAIN OF EVENT

Understanding how the pattern of your chain of events unfolds is a fantastic move forward on your road to recovery as you work through the steps. The roundabout will begin to slow down as you become aware of your specific chain and the significant changes you can make.

Your very first step in changing your whole pattern is NOW. STOP restricting your food. It is possible, and you can do this now!

HOW DOES IT ALL BEGIN? ... WITH DIETING!

This is where you need to break your chain of events. Because if you're dieting and depriving yourself of food or not eating at all, your metabolism will be working very sluggishly. You'll be more vulnerable to your bingeing and purging cycle. Your triggers will be heightened, and your thoughts will be excessively negative.

In simple terms, your body needs to function correctly by getting food and nutrients, but when your whole body becomes deprived of food, then the tension and the never-ending stream of thoughts about eating come. Your triggers become amplified, which then intensifies your urges, causing you to binge and purge.

Therefore, if you aren't eating healthily, you'll never break through your chains, and the roundabout will never slow, let alone stop. But if you change the first step, then you can change the whole chain of events, and how exciting it would be.

As you work through the book, there is a variety of different techniques to help you to begin to break this essential first step in breaking your patterns.

In step 4, you'll be beginning to introduce your structured eating program to help you with learning how you're going to stop dieting and restricting your food and start to eat healthily.

"NOW IS THE TIME TO TAKE CONTROL OF YOUR EATING RATHER THAN IT TAKING CONTROL OF YOU!" —KATE HUDSON-HALL

"SHRINK AND BLINK" TECHNIQUE

I know, for many, the idea of starting to eat and keep food in your stomach can bring up many distressing thoughts. One fantastic technique to reduce your negative thoughts about starting to introduce healthy eating is with the "Shrink and Blink Technique."

When you're aware of a painful thought and image, this is a simple yet super powerful way to work with your imagination and thoughts, to free you from them.

Are you ready? Listen up…

1. Think about a negative thought and the image that's connected to this thought.
2. Now put a frame around it and send it off into the distance. Notice it shrinking down into a small picture, like a postage stamp, or a single dot.
3. Blink it on and off black and white super-fast like a strobe light.

4. Do it again. Then keep doing it whenever difficult thoughts pop into your mind.

 Excellent! so keep blink, blink, blinking.

Video Demonstration Link: https://bulimiasucks.com/shrink-blink/

(Taken from *The NLP Toolbox* by Colin G. Smith)

YOUR BUBBLING CAULDRON OF AUTOMATIC THOUGHTS

Oh, these darn thoughts, especially if you're thinking about starting to eat healthily and keep food in your stomach. I get it, but we aren't always conscious of what we think, as we never usually pay attention to our thoughts; they're just there, bubbling in the background. They can become very self-critical, but we just tend to believe that our thoughts are factual.

But this bubbling cauldron of automatic thoughts is your interpretation of what's going on around you, rather than real facts. They depend on what life is like for you right now.

If you're happy and feel good about yourself, then your thoughts will indicate this and be positive and encouraging. But if you're feeling low and sad, your thoughts will show this and be gloomy and unenthusiastic.

Do you know how many thoughts you have each day?

It's approximately 60,000 each day, and most of those are linked to feelings! For people in general, 80% of daily thoughts are negative! Arrrrrrr, when I first heard this, I thought, *This surely can't be true.* But listen for yourself. Do you consistently beat yourself up? Is that voice in your head continually putting you down, telling you that you're no good? Probably.

Think back to your whole day and all your enormously debilitating beastly thoughts. These can be challenging to have and harder to feel, such as hopelessness, regret, shame, or loneliness. So, it's no wonder you end up trying to free yourself of these thoughts, even if it's only for a very brief period.

AWARENESS IS THE FIRST STEP TO BREAK THE CYCLE

WHAT ARE TRIGGERS?

Your triggers are anything that sends you into your pattern of binge-ing and purging. You would either:

Say something to yourself.
Make a picture in your mind.
Have a feeling.

It's something we don't usually pay attention to, and it happens in a flash. The thought will be brief, the image will be a quick flash, or the feeling will pop up and then disappear.

For example:

Think now about having your morning coffee or tea, hot water with lemon, or whatever you have. So how you get from not thinking about having your drink to having it? What do you think about just before you decide to have a coffee?

You may say to yourself, "It's time for my morning coffee!"
You may have a picture in your head of you drinking your coffee.
You may have a feeling you would like your coffee.

What's the very first thing you would do?

You'll have your very own specific triggers. So, what you need to do is begin to identify them. What precisely causes you to go from feeling okay to suddenly thinking or feeling about bingeing? Do you have any idea right now?

IT'S TIME TO **LISTEN... TO YOU.**

By spending more time listening to how you're talking to yourself, the more chance you have of changing these thoughts to more positive, self-empowering ones.

IT IS NOW TIME TO IDENTIFY YOUR OWN SPECIFIC TRIGGERS

Remember: Your body needs food, and cravings are justified, any sight or smell of food will be a trigger that you can't ignore. So, the first step is to eat.

Then once you're following your structured eating program, your triggers would be your next step in your chain of events.

HOW TO IDENTIFY YOUR TRIGGERS

So, I want you to begin to identify what your triggers are. Remember, it's the very first thing you do before you fall into that pattern of bingeing and purging. Finding out what your triggers are is the next most crucial step. Finding the trigger is a huge key to change.

Your triggers could be external, which might be:

- Something you see, maybe at work someone eating a sandwich? An unhelpful magazine headline, a seductive image of food on the cover, or seeing the calorie counts listed on a restaurant menu. It could be anything you SEE.
- Something you hear, maybe someone talking about food, or how happy they are, or the sound of someone eating a packet of crisps. It could be anything you HEAR.
- Something you touch, maybe handing someone some food, or someone gave you that packet of crisps, or you were touching your stomach. It could be anything you TOUCH.
- Something you taste, maybe having a coffee and how you would love a biscuit to go with that, or someone gave you one crisp from their crisp packet. It could be anything you TASTE.
- Something you smell, tantalizing aromas wafting as you walk past bakers or the smell of someone cooking. It could be anything you SMELL.

Your triggers could be internal or mental, which might be:

- Something you might be thinking in your head such as an image of you bingeing or purging, an image of you struggling to pull up your jeans, or an image of you standing on the scales looking deflated.
- Something you might be saying to yourself such as "I've had such a stressful day, and I'm hungry, I need to go on a binge"; "I need to lose weight, and my jeans are too tight"; or "This book isn't going to *really help me*. I've had bulimia for such a long time. I'm a hopeless case." (But, oh my, how wrong you would be! So keep reading.)
- Something you might be feeling such as hopeless, helpless, lonely, sad, bored, upset, guilty, worthless, and the list goes on.

For me, my pattern would be:

I'd first have a feeling of being lonely. Secondly, I'd have an image of me bingeing. Lastly, I'd have a thought, *I'm so sad.*

 The most important point we can learn here is that the internal triggers that cause your painful feelings are all in your head; they aren't real! Your physical trigger of true hunger, now that's real.

"DON'T BELIEVE EVERYTHING YOU THINK."

You can begin to change right here, right now; it's possible to change these old behaviors into new positive behaviors.

But first, you need to understand what your specific triggers are. What's the first thing that happens to send you down that road of bingeing and purging?

I want you now to sit back and think about what your triggers might be. Begin to break down the pattern of what gets you zipping down into that bulimia spiral.

 Complete the IDENTIFY YOUR TRIGGERS table in Step 2, in your workbook.

Otherwise, grab your notebook and answer these questions:

What do you see?

What do you hear?

What do you taste?

What do you think to yourself?

What images do you have?

What you touch?

What do you smell?

What feelings are you having?

Once you've identified your first trigger, then you can begin to make the change to that trigger. So, read on to find out how.

HOW TO CHANGE YOUR TRIGGERS INSTANTLY WITH "THE INSTANT TRIGGER CHANGE" TECHNIQUE

I am now going to show you how you can learn to change your triggers instantly with this NLP (Neuro-linguistic Programming) technique.

Oh, yes, this is where it gets inspiring.

So, find a quiet place and sit down: now, I want you to take each trigger you have identified, and for each trigger, follow the instructions below.

Read through all the steps, so you know where you're going with this.

1. Think about your first trigger that sends you down into your negative pattern of bingeing and purging. It could be an image of you slumped on your bed feeling worthless and lonely, or a thought similar to "My jeans are too damn tight this morning."

2. Imagine a movie starting from this point and immediately white it out, make the movie screen completely blank, white.

3. Replace the image immediately with an image or a movie of yourself engaging in a new positive behavior, looking happy, and being free from your bulimia. This could be an image or movie of you walking in a park or on a beach, feeling healthier and more positive about yourself. It will allow you to attach the trigger to the thought of you being free from the pattern.

4. Repeat Steps 1 - 3, a few times on the first trigger and notice yourself seeing differently about that trigger, bingeing and purging.

5. Repeat Steps 1—4, with the next trigger you have identi-
    fied, then continue working through your list.

 This is a fantastic tool to break your pattern between
the triggers and the pattern of bingeing and purging.
So, go ahead and give it a try; it's so simple yet incredibly powerful (Bandler, 2010).

Video Demonstration Link: http://bulimiasucks.com/instant-trigger-change/

"ITS NOT SO MUCH WHERE YOU STAND AS IN
WHAT DIRECTION YOU ARE MOVING IN"

ELTON JOHN has overcome many addictions, including bulimia.

He isn't ashamed of the problems he's had in the past; they've only
made him stronger. "I was cocaine-addicted. I was an alcoholic. I
had a sexual addiction. I was bulimic for six years," he told the *Mirror*
in 2019. "It was all through being paranoid about my weight but not
able to stop eating. So, in the end, I'd gorge, then make myself sick"
(Firman, 2020).

STEP 2 - HERE ARE YOUR KEY
EMPOWERING ACTION STEPS:

Now is the time you can start to feel proud of yourself for having
read through and taken the vital first action steps to begin to slow
down your merry-go-round and change the way you're thinking
and feeling about yourself and where you were.

*   Now you've created your motivation with the "ELECTRIFY
    YOUR MOTIVATION" TECHNIQUE. It's essential to keep your-

self motivated using your new motivational anchor. Press index finger and thumb together, then keep going over the technique to help to reinforce the inspiration you need to take the bull by the horns and continue on your incredible new pathway to breaking the old links and chains to freedom.

- Now you have a clearer understanding of how your bulimic pattern and triggers are connected to the tormenting urges to binge and purge. You can begin to break this pattern.
- Thinking about your triggers, learn what your specific steps are. Is it a thought, feeling, or image first? Write a list of all your triggers as they happen.
- Continue working with "THE INSTANT TRIGGER CHANGE TECHNIQUE" on new triggers that suddenly appear from around each corner.

You've learned a lot about your eating triggers here in Step 2 and how your thoughts and feelings are all connected to your uncontrollable behaviors.

These are exciting steps of learning about you!

STEP 3

WHY DO I HAVE THIS HUGE OVERWHELMING URGE TO BINGE?

"DON'T WAIT FOR YOUR FEELINGS TO CHANGE TO TAKE ACTION. TAKE ACTION, AND YOUR FEELINGS WILL CHANGE."

Your empowering learnings from Step 2:

- Right now, how motivated are you? If you aren't feeling super motivated to learn about taking this next step. It's essential to go back and rerun "The Electrify Your Motivation" technique from Step 2 over and over again. I want you charged up and excited to move on to focus powerfully on this next step.
- So, you've learned and understood the pattern of this never-ending bulimic roundabout and how your triggers drive you to binge and purge and then leave you with uncontrollable feelings of guilt, shame, disgust, in a continuous loop swirling around and around in your head.
- Discovering how you can change your triggers is incredibly powerfully with the "Instant trigger change" technique.

If any new trigger springs from nowhere, you can change that trigger instantly.

The positive guidance you'll be learning here in Step 3:

- Now that you're becoming more aware of the triggers that drive your negative behavior, you're going to take a more in-depth look at the thoughts linked to your triggers that that then drive that urge and what you can start to do differently to begin to break this pattern.
- Once you've become more aware of your urges to binge, you'll be taking a closer look at the space between your thoughts, feelings, unbearable urges, and your bingeing. This will help you realize that, even though the urges are automatic, the behavior is not.

You'll then also be learning how you can begin, rather than trying to push away your urges, to turn toward them. Going with the sensations, you're thinking, feeling, and riding them just like a professional surfer skimming the waves. With a marvelous technique called urge surfing!

 The reason you have this overwhelming urge to binge is because you're restricting your food, but when you stop and provide your body with eating regularly, then the binge urge means nothing = zilch!

What we've learned so far is that your dieting leads to your cravings. Then, when triggered, in comes your powerful binge voice and agonizing feelings that suddenly explode into your urges to binge and purge.

**DIETING leads to CRAVINGS,
which leads to your TRIGGERS
and then the BINGE VOICE starts shouting,
which leads to your uncontrollable URGES**

For example, something would trigger me (I had a mountain of triggers), and then the screaming thoughts would start, such as *I'm such a bad person* and *I'm stupid*. Then along came the feelings of hopelessness, loneliness, and sadness connected with these thoughts. I felt there was no way I could control them. Then along came my urges, which were suffocating, fueling an uncontrollable need to feast on any food I could find. It was as if I had the devil inside of me.

The only way I knew how to deal with all these uncontrollable thoughts and feelings and the enormous urges was to make myself feel a little better if only for a short period and binge and purge.

Although I didn't actually need to binge and give in to these urges, my survival mechanism took over; I had to free myself of so many painful, tormenting feelings and thoughts.

This is what we've learned about your pattern so far...

RESTRICTING YOUR FOOD INTAKE ➡

CAUSES TENSION AND CRAVINGS ➡

WHICH THEN

INTENSIFIES YOUR TRIGGERS ➡

CREATING YOUR NEGATIVE THOUGHTS ➡

YOUR IRRATIONAL THOUGHTS

Let's take a closer look at these darn thoughts.

BUT EVERYWHERE YOU LOOK...THERE IS FOOD!

Food is available all the time; wherever you look, there's food! Whether that be on a billboard, shop window, or TV. Of course, then there it is in your fridge and cupboards; you feel surrounded by these food triggers.

Continue to identify what your triggers are from Step 2. For some people, the first link in their trigger could be what they're thinking to themselves. It's that whispering voice in their head, which I liken to a little evil green leprechaun. Others call it "the eating disorders voice" or the "binge voice." Some of my clients benefit from calling him "ED" (eating disorder). But you could call him whatever you like! I prefer an evil leprechaun and imagined him super glued onto my shoulder, hissing viciousness, which then caused my unbearable feelings. In recovery, I would slap him off my shoulder to stop the constant berating.

Let's be honest. He's more than likely whispering hurtful comments 24 hours a day, but if you had a choice and met the beast, you wouldn't want the little monster in your life even for a minute. He can be so controlling and dominant, and he's also very conniving and tries to trick you into believing what he tells you. "If you lose more weight, then you'll be happy, and life will be perfect." But whatever you do, it won't be good enough. He'll always come back, bullying you into bingeing again.

But it's difficult not to listen or believe in what he has to say, and whenever you try to do something positive in your life, there he's telling you, "That's not good enough. You had an apple earlier, and you're going to get fat, then no one will love you. You shouldn't have eaten anything; you might as well go on a binge. Go on, go on, this will be your last binge, and then tomorrow, you'll stop. You're all alone for two hours, plenty of time for a binge. You're worthless and don't deserve to be happy."

 This leprechaun isn't part of you; he may sound like you, but he isn't in you. Imagine he's your bullying bulimia voice sitting on your shoulder. He's a little shriveling leprechaun that may seem to shout louder than your real voice, but he's still an outsider.

Your real voice, that positive, healthy part of you, is still there, maybe buried beneath your leprechaun, but if you listen carefully, you'll be able to hear it.

"IF YOU WOULDN'T SAY IT TO A FRIEND, THEN DON'T SAY IT TO YOURSELF"

DO YOU HAVE A SPADE? BECAUSE NOW IS THE TIME TO DIG OUT YOUR REAL VOICE

 It's time to dig out your real voice and learn to separate the leprechaun's toxic whispering from your authentic voice and listen for your healthy voice. Over time, it will gradually become louder. As this happens, believe what it says and embrace it. Allow it room to flourish, giving you confidence and strength, as it develops, to begin talking back to the leprechaun.

So, this little irritating green evil leprechaun and his constant negative chatter doesn't stop with its nonsense. But what we can learn here is that he's just a bully with a voice, and by connecting with your true self, you can gain back control of your life and begin to recover fully. It's your life, not the toxic leprechaun's!

 Complete the REAL VOICE, YOUR CHOICE table in Step 3, in your workbook. Otherwise, grab your notebook and complete the questions below and start now to listen for your real voice with curiosity to help you become more aware of your own voice.

ASK YOURSELF: **YOUR REAL VOICE:**

Can you hear it in words or sounds?

What sort of tone does it have?

Is it a high or low pitch?

Is it constant or intermittent?

Which direction does it come from?

How loud is it? When you hear it, could you make it any louder?

What happens if you imagine turning up the volume?

Excellent! You want to make your own voice as prominent as possible; curiosity is your first step in this exercise and learning the difference between your binge voice and your authentic, healthy voice.

WHAT FEELINGS DOES YOUR LEPRECHAUN CREATE?

 Your thoughts are linked to your feelings, BUT he's NOT the binge event itself; he's causing your negative feelings that then drive your urge to binge.

Let's think about what feelings you may be having because, whatever you do, they don't go away until you binge and purge.

 Complete the FEELINGS table in Step 3, in your workbook. Otherwise, grab your notebook and complete the list below

So begin today, making a list for you to:

- Start to become more aware of what your feelings are for you.
- Then begin to learn to change as you go on to learn the different techniques in this book.

FOR EXAMPLE:	LIST YOUR OWN FEELINGS:

Anxious

Comfort

Lonely

Stressed

Panic

Ashamed

Oh yes, and a multitude more on top, so keep adding to your list.

THE SEPARATION

As I mentioned, let's imagine that your binge voice was the ugly green leprechauns, not the binge pattern itself. He's the source of the thoughts that drive your feelings that then create your urges before you binge. And just because the leprechaun is whispering in your ear, "You feel so lonely; go on have a binge, eat that bar of chocolate in the cupboard. It'll make you feel better," he isn't actually the physical binge itself.

THE CHOICE WITH THAT VOICE

Just because the leprechaun is whispering nonsense in your ear that causes you so many horrific feelings, you don't have to listen to him. What if you ignored him? Yes, you wouldn't binge.

HOW TO BECOME MORE AWARE OF YOUR URGE BINGE PATTERN

It's essential to recognize that the leprechaun is just a voice. He's NOT the binge event itself; he's the urge to binge.

 The further we can separate between the two, put distance between the leprechaun's chatter and the feelings of panic and the binge, the more we can begin to change this habit.

ITS TIME TO FIND YOUR SPACE BETWEEN YOUR URGES AND BINGEING

Once you've become more aware of your leprechaun's evil words and your urges to binge, take a closer look at the space between the two. It will help you realize that, even though the urges are automatic, your behavior isn't.

There's always at least a moment or, as I call it, a "space" between. When can you choose differently and learn to be more accepting of your urges to binge?

By separating between:

Your toxic	S	
leprechaun and his	P	
muttering that	A	**That then causes your**
causes your negative	C	**binge.**
feelings, which are	E	
your urges.		

The two are separate. There's space between.

Of course, over time, this has become a habit. That little green irritating leprechaun is firmly holding on; it's as if he has his claws gripping your shoulder, and this pattern becomes a regular habit. The good news is that you have a choice and can learn to change your habits.

Let's look again at your bulimic cycle.

YOUR BULIMIC CYCLE INCLUDING YOUR SPACE BETWEEN:

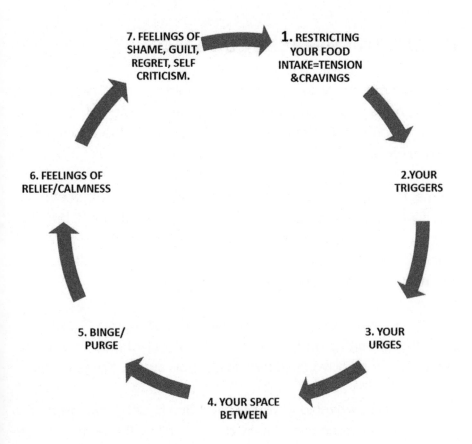

7. FEELINGS OF SHAME, GUILT, REGRET, SELF CRITICISM.

1. RESTRICTING YOUR FOOD INTAKE=TENSION &CRAVINGS

6. FEELINGS OF RELIEF/CALMNESS

2.YOUR TRIGGERS

5. BINGE/ PURGE

3. YOUR URGES

4. YOUR SPACE BETWEEN

This diagram shows where exactly "a space" is between your urges and your binges.

The only reason you binge is to remove your uncomfortable "urges to binge." If you could learn to be more accepting of your binge urges, they wouldn't cause you as much bother. Then you would be in a better position to ignore them.

As long as you've stopped restricting your food and providing your body with eating regularly, then the binge urge means nothing = zilch!

ITS TIME TO EMBRACE YOUR SPACE

Often, we get swept away with the thoughts and feelings of panic and the habit of bingeing and act on our urges immediately. But the more you can understand your specific patterns, the easier it is to begin to change it.

For me, I thought the leprechaun would shout so loudly that eventually, it would spring to life and beat me to death! It didn't, but I felt powerless. If I had learned to sit with the panic feelings, realize that nothing actually happened, that I was okay, my life didn't end, the fear hadn't killed me, then I wouldn't have binged.

Your binge urge is just patterns of thinking and feeling. They're like any other thoughts and feelings, and it's your choice to listen to them. They don't have the power to control you; you have a choice.

- So, however loud your leprechaun is, and however strong your feelings are, slowly begin to allow the feelings to be there, choosing to accept them.

- Continually resist what your leprechaun and your feelings are telling you to do. Instead, tell yourself, "I can cope with these thoughts and feelings."
- See how long you can sit with them; start with 30 seconds, continually repeating, "I can cope with these thoughts and feelings." Then, once you've cemented your 30 seconds and can ignore the negativity, extend the length of time and build from there.

The longer you can sit with your urges and your space in-between rather than act on them. The sooner they'll become less intense and loosen their grip on you. Giving you even more space between your urges and your binge. Over time, they'll begin to reduce and eventually dissolve.

WHAT IS AN URGE?

An urge is an uncontrollable "need" to binge. It's a knowing that if you were to binge and purge briefly, yes, you'll get a reprieve or a moment's break from all the disheartening thoughts and feelings. It's your way, at that moment, of freeing yourself from all your unbearable feelings.

I know I keep mentioning this, but it's a crucial point to make... when addressing your urges, if you're following your structured eating program (which we'll discuss in Step 4). Eating healthily, giving your body the right amount of the correct healthy nutrients that will provide you with so much more control of your triggers and urges.

As you know, the more you try to push the leprechaun away, the louder and bigger his voice will become. Then the difficulty, if you don't ignore it, will blow up like a giant balloon stretched to its limit and explode into an uncontrollable bingeing frenzy, and the whole habitual pattern begins again. So, what if you decided to turn toward the problematic thoughts and feelings rather than trying to fight them?

"LIFE OFFERS YOU SO MANY DOORS. IT IS UP TO YOU WHICH ONE TO OPEN AND WHICH ONE TO CLOSE"

YOU ARE DOING SO WELL, SO KEEP GOING... IT'S TIME TO DELVE DEEPER INTO YOUR URGES

Let's identify the specific pattern of your urges by tuning in and becoming aware of all the thoughts and feelings connected to your URGES. Fill these questions out over the next week; think about your urges and how they drive you to binge.

As you work through answering these questions, you're not trying to resolve anything. You're only trying to understand your urges clearer.

 Complete the DELVE INTO YOUR URGES table in Step 3, in your workbook. Otherwise, grab your notebook and answer these questions:

ASK YOURSELF: **LIST YOUR ANSWERS:**

WHAT DO YOUR URGES
FEEL LIKE TO YOU?

WHAT PHYSICAL SYMPTOMS
DO YOUR URGES CREATE?

WHEN DO YOUR URGES OCCUR?
HOW OFTEN?

DO THE URGES HAVE A VOICE
THAT ENCOURAGES YOU TO BINGE?
WHAT DOES THAT VOICE SAY TO YOU?

DOES THE VOICE OF THE URGE
USE PRECISE REASONS TO GET
YOU TO BINGE?
LIST AS MANY AS YOU CAN?

WHAT DOES THE VOICE OF
THE URGE PROMISE YOU?
WHAT PAYOFF OR REWARDS DOES IT PROMISE
IF YOU FOLLOW THROUGH AND BINGE?

WRITE DOWN ANYTHING ELSE YOU
NOTICE ABOUT YOUR URGES:

Sometimes, your urges to binge can be very faint, as if in the far distance. So, completing the questions to learn a lot about your urges and your own leprechaun's whispering. Excellent!

Some of my clients feel they go on a binge without much thought. It just happens. But this is never the case, and there's always a pattern. Your triggers cause your thoughts and feelings, which then surge into your urges with a panic and binge and purge.

Don't worry about accepting or dismissing the urges for the moment; just set your sights on being able to identify an urge when it comes up and sitting in the space between your urges and your binge. Each time this happens, stretching the time out, gradually lengthening your space. Continue this for a week and then come back to this page and carry on reading how you can further address your urges.

SO NOW, I WANT TO TEACH YOU ANOTHER WAY TO WORK WITH YOUR URGES

Okay, so now, you've spent time sitting in the space between your urges. I want to teach you another technique to address your urges. Here we go… This is exciting…

MINDFULNESS

Learning to introduce mindfulness in everyday life will be an incredibly powerful pathway to give you a break from your evil leprechaun's chatter. It's learning to pay attention, in the present moment, with purpose and nonjudgmentally. It's as simple as that!

We're hardly ever in the present moment. We're either worrying about the past or thinking about what might happen in the future. If we were to hear a loud bang outside or see a beautiful view, this would bring us back into the present. Here and now is where we want to be.

It's like pressing the pause button of your mind, giving you a break from the constant, never-ending chatter in your mind

Much research has been carried out on the multiple benefits of mindfulness and eating disorders, particularly bulimia. Studies show it can relieve several psychological and physical issues. For example:

- Obsessive thoughts
- Stress
- Anxiety
- Depression
- Low self-esteem
- Chronic pain
- Insomnia
- Lower blood pressure

My clients with an eating disorder whom I've taught mindfulness also found it hugely beneficial for:

- Cultivating self-compassion
- Building a strong sense of self-awareness and self-identity
- Mindfulness eating

FINDING FREEDOM FROM YOUR DEVIOUS LEPRECHAUN WITH THE MINDFULNESS TECHNIQUE CALLED: "URGE SURFING"

WHAT IS URGE SURFING AND HOW CAN IT HELP YOU RIGHT NOW?

Now you have an awareness of mindfulness and a further understanding of your patterns that create these urges and spent time sitting in your space between them; you're now going to take this further with learning to surf those urges to binge.

Alan Marlatt, a psychologist and pioneer in the area of alcohol addiction, developed urge surfing from mindfulness. We can learn to take back control over how we react to our urges. They aren't dangerous and won't kill us; they're just feelings.

Let me explain. How often, when you're trying to control yourself and not binge, you consciously try to distract yourself by watching TV or spending time on your phone playing a game? Does this distraction work for you?

Urge surfing is sitting with that urge, using your breath and attention to ride the wave out, turning toward it rather than fighting it, going with the sensations you're thinking and feeling and riding them just like a professional surfer rides the waves. So rather than trying to distract yourself from your unbearable urges, ride with them; allow them to be there.

Your urges are similar to a wave that sweeps over you. It starts as a ripple in a calm seabed. Then as it slowly drifts forward, builds up, becoming bigger and bigger until it finally crashes over onto the seashore then calmly recedes. It continually returns in this nev-er-ending cycle.

We might not have control over the enormous urge or 15-foot wave right now, but we can learn to surf it, go with it, as we do have con-trol over how we react to it.

TIME TO LEARN THIS FANTASTIC SKILL OF URGE SURFING

 You may not *find this easy*, so it's essential to be kind and compassionate with yourself because, instead of trying not to think about the unbearable urge to binge, you will turn toward the urge and stay closely with it. It's about getting to know it, sitting with it, and feeling it.

The key is to build up your confidence. Let's be honest. You wouldn't jump from a boat into the sea to go surfing if you couldn't swim. First, you need some lessons.

Before we begin the exact steps on how to urge surf, let's start with less intense urges. I want you now to think about an urge you had recently, preferably not one connected with food, maybe some-thing like looking at social media on your phone or checking an email or text message.

Find a quiet, comfortable place, have your phone nearby so you can see it.

Look at your phone and imagine an important text has come in (turn notifications off, so it's easier to imagine the important text coming in. If notifications are on, you will know that no text has come in). The urge to read it increases, so tune in and make this urge as clear as possible and then see if you can become aware of all the different sensations that come forward.

 Complete the URGE SURFING LEARNINGS (Part 1) table in Step 3, in your workbook. Otherwise, grab your notebook and answer these questions:

ASK YOURSELF: **YOUR ANSWERS:**

How does it make you feel?

Where in the body is that feeling?

How intense is it?

Does it have a color?

What thoughts are you having?

Do you have an image in your
mind of the urge?

Stay with all these sensations and notice how they change over time. Use your breath to help you breathe through this. Simply focus on your breathing, noticing each breath as your breath in and out.

 Wow, there you go, you did it. You have successfully broken through your first urge.

Usually, an urge lasts for 20 minutes. Giving in to your urges makes them even more powerful. This is the last thing you want right now.

So, if you were to sit with your urge, many negative thoughts and feelings of panic and fear could come up that may intensify the urge. It could be a thought like *I'm scared,* or *I'm a failure* that makes it even more powerful. These will eventually gradually subside, but they'll take a lot longer than if you learned to urge surf.

ARE YOU READY TO SURF THAT URGE?

Here we go, below are the steps to begin to break this pattern of unbearable urges connected to your bulimia. Remember, you need to build up your confidence.

Step 1

Let's practice mindfulness. Find a quiet, comfortable place where you won't be disturbed. Close your eyes and, with your mouth closed, focus your attention on your breathing. Feel the air coming in through your nostrils, your chest lifting and falling, your stomach rising and falling. Focus on all aspects of your breathing, and if you notice your mind wandering off and thinking about something else, kindly, not judgmentally, bring it back to your breath.

Do this for approximately two minutes. To help you focus on your breathing, think to yourself as you inhale, *breath in*, and exhale with *breath out*.

(If this all becomes too much and you are worried that by thinking about your urge it may bring on a binge, then focus on your breathing, the air coming in through your nose, your chest and stomach rising and falling, and stay with your breath until you feel ready to focus again on your urge.)

Alternatively, zip back to your phone urge, checking a text, as you need to build up your confidence first with this technique).

Step 2

When you're ready, in your mind's eye, imagine a difficult situation that causes the urge to binge, then simply sit back and notice:

Where in the body do you feel the unbearable urge? For some, it may be their stomach or chest.

If you're struggling to connect with your urge, then think back to a time when you had an urge that was related to your bulimia.

The reason we breathe in and out through our nose when practicing mindfulness is that it helps to calm and ground the mind. But if your nose is stuffed with a cold or allergies, by all means, breathe through the mouth).

Step 3

Once you're aware of where in the body you feel the unbearable urge, become aware of the sensations connected to your urge, and just observe them.

 Complete the URGE SURFING LEARNINGS (Part 2) table in Step 3, in your workbook. Otherwise, grab your notebook and answer these questions:

This time, write in more detail about your urges.

ASK YOURSELF: **YOUR ANSWERS:**

What does it feel like?

Pressure? Tension?

Tingly? Warm or cool?

Where in the body is that feeling?

How intense is it?

How big is it?

Does it move, or is it still?

Does it have a color?

What thoughts are you having?

Do you have an image in your mind of the urge?

Notice how the urges are like waves. They slowly build, come to a peak, and crash down. Stay with the event for as long as you can. It's best to start with five minutes and just observe the waves. Even though you aren't responding at this moment, the urges lessen and floats away. Look at you like a real surfer riding the wave.

The urge may change. Some may be a little swell, others may be a massive tidal wave, but stay with whatever comes up. Surf, surf, surf.

Step 4

Bring your focus back to your urge and notice how it has changed. Becoming aware of all the sensations.

Imagine the wave as an unbearable urge and see if you can tune into it as it builds up and then eventually hits a peak, then falls and subsides. Imagine you're a professional surfer and use your breath to help you to ride the wave.

Stay with the sensations as they begin to build again, notice the peak, then be aware as it dissolves back down.

 As the wave begins to build, imagine you are standing on a surfboard and ride the waves.

Great, you're a real surfer; you've done it! Congratulations! You can be present, experience your urges, and not react. You now have begun to break free from that urge. Fabulous!

Whenever you feel the unbearable urge beginning to build, take time out, and start surfing your urges. In the beginning, see how long you can stay with it, set a timer, start with five minutes, then build up to ten minutes, then fifteen minutes and so on.

I would like you to practice your new skill of urge surfing at least twice a day and work up to four times a day. Over time, you'll become a professional surfer. The urges to binge become easier to surf, and as this happens, you'll feel excited that you're beginning to take control of your life.

Video Demonstration Link: https://bulimiasucks.com/urge-surfing/

NICOLE SCHERZINGER - American singer, says:

"I can empathize so much with people who have demons and voices in their heads, who aren't nice to themselves. It robs you of living your life," she says. "But you can recover, and you can get rid of it forever. I did it, and that's why it's so important for me to share my story. You hide it from the world, and you isolate yourself. But you can beat it. Don't give up because you're so special, and you're meant for such great things" (Olivares, 2014).

Here are your action steps to focus on:

Wow, all this learning, I want you to feel proud you're taking action and beginning to change. Look at you breaking the old way of thinking, your habits, and patterns, and stepping outside of your comfort zone. It may not be easy, but as you begin to notice your behavior changing, you'll feel so empowered.

STEP 3 - HERE ARE YOUR KEY EMPOWERING ACTION STEPS:

- Learn your patterns, what your triggers are. Those affect your thoughts, which then create the urges that cause your binges.
- Pay more attention to your own devious leprechaun on your shoulder, what it's saying to you that drives you toward your urges to binge.
- As you progressively become aware of your leprechaun's whisperings, that then drives the urges to binge. You'll realize that even though the urges are automatic, the behavior is not. You always have a moment, a space between your

urges and the binge. Learning to sit in this moment with mindfulness will begin to help you to break your pattern.

- Now you can surf like a real professional, stay committed to working through the steps twice a day, and building from there.

- As you learn to break free from your urges, how motivated are you to move onto the next step? If you aren't really inspired, then squeeze your left index finger and thumb to feel incredibly motivated.

Fantastic, you have now completed Step 3 and beginning to break this cycle of bingeing and purging. You're exceptional, and I'm even more proud of you today, and you should be too. These are huge steps, as you're taking back control of your deserved life.

What a great inspiration you are to others.

"IF WE ARE READY TO TEAR DOWN THE WALL THAT CONFINES US, BREAK THE CHAINS THAT IMPRISON US, WE WILL DISCOVER WHAT OUR WINGS ARE FOR"—MICHAEL ELMORE-MEEGAN

STEP 4

HOW DO I EAT LIKE A NORMAL PERSON?

"THE DAY YOU PLANT THE SEED IS NOT THE DAY YOU EAT THE FRUIT" —FABIENNE FREDRICKSON

Your empowering learnings from Step 3:

- Having begun to open up and understand that your triggers cause your thoughts and feelings that impel your urges, driving you to binge and purge, is an incredible step forward toward real permanent recovery.
- As you become aware of your patterns, you'll realize that even though the urges are automatic, your behavior is not; there's a choice. Gradually, you're becoming aware of a space between your urges and binges. Stretching this space will give you the power to take a different path.
- By using your new skills of urge surfing, turning toward your urges and loosening their grip, it will become easier to let them go and not allow them to drive you to binge and purge.

The positive guidance you'll be learning here in Step 4:

- This step is all about introducing your structured eating program. As you've learned so far, restricting your foods leads to your cravings. (Uh oh, here I go again!) Then, when triggered, in slithers your evil leprechaun voice bringing with it a sack load of painful feelings that can suddenly explode into your uncontrollable urges, which lead you to binge and purge or overexercise.
- Once you've established your structured eating program, you can then start to introduce your intuitive eating plan. You'll learn to tune in to only eating when you're hungry, eating slowly, and becoming aware of the satisfying feeling when your body knows you've eaten enough, and you can stop eating.
- How motivated are you right now? If you aren't feeling really motivated to take this next step, go back and rerun the motivation technique from Step 2 over and over again to charge you up to get you super-empowered to focus on this next step.

HOW DO I EAT LIKE A NORMAL PERSON?

Recovering from bulimia means you need to begin to relearn how to eat like a normal person. At this stage of recovery, many of my clients have no idea what to eat or where to begin. So, I'm going to teach you how to do this with a structured eating program.

In this crucial change you're about to make, you're going to learn why it's soooo darn important not to skip this step. It's time to take your whole past negative thinking and chuck it out the window!

Begin a fresh new page on how you're going to move forward free from your old pattern of thinking, feeling, and behaving.

"LET'S TAKE YOUR RECOVERY ONE BITE AT A TIME"

HOW WILL I COPE WITH FOOD IN MY STOMACH?

Let's talk about how it will feel to have food in your stomach when you begin the positive pattern of eating again. There's a possibility you could get stomach sensitivities. I'm reluctant to mention these, but just so you're aware, these could be diarrhea, constipation, pain, nausea, and bloating. Therefore, you may gain weight, but this is usually due to the "bulimia bloat," which is a common symptom of recovery as your body adjusts and balances. (See more information on weight gain and the bulimia bloat in Step 6.)

 So, it may not be a very comfortable feeling, to begin with, and it may take time for your body to return to its normal physical process. **But your body will adjust to this.**

Your body has been working hard without the right nutrients to take care of you. But once it understands there's regular intake of food, this will speed up your metabolism, moving the foods through your body more efficiently. But if you decrease the meals, it will then slow it down again. So, one vital key to learn is not to reduce the amount of food you eat.

Right now, you may be feeling overwhelmed with the huge step you're about to take, but your bulimia didn't suddenly happen. It was a pattern that took a while to develop, and your body will take time to adjust, level out, and heal itself.

I know this can sound all too overwhelming, but your body needs to have regular nutrients to balance out its natural chemistry. It will eventually stop sending those craving messages to your brain that send you into the downward spiral of binges.

SO, WHAT HAPPENS WHEN YOU RESTRICT YOUR FOODS OR INCREASE YOUR LAXATIVES OR DIURETICS?...(Oh yes, I'm allowed to repeat myself in this step, as it's all about learning to eat like all those "normal" people!)

Apart from the fact that your body needs the food to work healthily, restricting your food intake or an increase in your laxatives or diuretics will cause:

Physical hunger:

- Your energy levels will plummet.
- You'll become dehydrated.
- Your heart rate decreases.
- Your metabolism slows and you quickly convert the calories you do absorb into fat stores, and the list goes on.

Emotional hunger:

- Increase your obsession with foods and eating.
- You'll forever worry about what you should and shouldn't eat.
- You'll become sensitive even to smell food.
- Your triggers will be heightened, and therefore more likely to give in and binge and purge, which could make you feel like a failure or depressed, irritable, and this list goes on and on!

Therefore, it's important to begin eating healthily again relearn how to eat normally.

I know how this may sound so scary to you right now. But beginning to eat again is the number one key.

THE BENEFITS OF YOUR STRUCTURED EATING

One of the most important steps you can take to break through your urges to binge is to introduce your structured eating program. By following your plan, you can expect a vast **50-80% reduction in your urges to binge**. Wahooooo! We like that.

The main benefits of a structured eating program are to:

- Provide your body with the wonderful nutrients it needs.
- Undo the damage of malnutrition.
- Reduce your urges to binge on food.
- Relearn how to eat like a normal person again.
- Rebalance your blood sugar levels, which will automatically control your appetite.
- Get your digestive system working for you correctly.
- Learning to stop restricting foods.
- Increase your metabolism; therefore, you'll feel full of energy.

OTHER PHYSICAL CHANGES

- Over time, bloating and water retention will reduce, and your weight will stabilize.
- Your throat won't be sore.

- No more swollen cheeks, puffy eyes, etc.
- You'll start to have regular bowel movements.
- Your menstrual cycle will gradually return.
- Bones will become stronger and healthier.
- Your heart, kidneys, blood pressure will all return to normal.

EMOTIONAL CHANGES

- Feel less anxious.
- Your self-esteem will improve.
- Feel so much calmer.
- Your confidence will flourish as your social life improves.
- Your emotions will stabilize.

The list is never-ending full of so many incredible positives; you'll be like a new you with so much energy.

HOW DO I START EATING AGAIN?

The way you're going to start to eat again is with a program that gives you a structure around food and retrains your mind and body to expect food often and regularly. By doing this, you're telling your body, "You don't have to force me to binge on large amounts of food now because I'll provide you with more food later."

 In the beginning, the more prepared you are, the less you'll have to think about food and what to eat, which will be a massive help, as, let's be honest, this may all seem not so easy.

So, get organized; start to:

- Plan your meals ahead of time. You may want to plan your meals for just a couple of days in advance or maybe the whole week.
- Plan what meals you're going to prepare and buy all the food for the week at one time—reducing the temptation to slip from your positive path.

This structured eating program is only temporary, as once you begin to feel more confident, you can get rid of the program.

WHAT WOULD BE A HEALTHY BALANCED MEAL?

Depending on your goals and how much you're moving your body, this information will vary from person to person. But these are general guides, and the division into thirds is by volume, with the aim at averaging the recommended portion. Also, reach out for support from a family member or friend and speak to a nutritionist, which would be a huge help at this time to guide you in the right direction.

The key to a healthy balanced meal, is to have a combination of:

One-third carbohydrates

One-third protein

One-third fruits or vegetables

(Think of it like this, dividing it into thirds)

Plus, eat some kind of fat. Fat adds flavor to your food and helps you to feel full.

Make sure your portions are proportionate and not too big or small.

Eating a wide variety of fresh foods from all the groups will stabilize erratic blood sugar levels and reduce the urge to binge.

It's important not to count calories when you start eating again, as this isn't helpful. Calorie counting is connected to dieting, and this is where we want to steer clear. It's time to let that negative pattern go. As you follow a structured meal plan, then you'll be getting all the right foods, and we can leave the calorie counting to other wannabes!

CARBOHYDRATES:

Carbohydrates provide most of the energy needed in our daily lives, both for normal body functions, such as breathing, heartbeat, digestion, and brain activity, and exercise. They also play a critical role in the production of serotonin (the happy hormone), which is the primary neurotransmitter regulating your mood and appetite. Carbs include sugar, starch, and fiber. So, when you deprive yourself of carbohydrates, you can put yourself at risk of lower serotonin levels, which, in turn, can affect your mood. (Lots more on serotonin in Step 6).

Types of carbohydrates to add to your meal plan:

Squash, corn, sweet or other potatoes, (yes, corn and potatoes are vegetables, but they also contain high levels of carbohydrates) brown rice, wholegrain bread and cereals, wholemeal bagels and pasta, beans, lentils, oats, etc.

PROTEIN:

Protein balances your blood sugar levels, which makes you feel fuller for longer, which then moderates your appetite and hugely helps to reduce those cravings.

Types of protein to add to your meal plan:

Seafood, fish, meats, eggs, beans.

FATS:

Eating fat is probably something you've tried to avoid at all costs, but fats actually help reduce weight, and they also:

Improve the absorption of essential nutrients.

Help you feel full.

Serve as reserves for energy storage.

Help to curb overeating.

 HOT TIP = at the start of your recovery, eating fat can help to reduce the initial "bulimia bloat."

There are many different types of fats:

Saturated fats: These are found in dairy products and meat.

Trans fats: These are found in cakes, biscuits, and snack foods.

(Try to avoid saturated and trans fats, as they are unhealthy).

Unsaturated fats: These are found in fish and plants.

Omega 3: Found in oily fish, including salmon, mackerel, and sardines. If you don't eat fish, then linseeds, pecans, flax seeds, and hazelnuts are also rich in omega 3. (If you've been abusing laxatives, avoid taking linseed and flax seeds, as they could cause loose stools; instead eat chia seeds).

Types of fats to add to your meal plan:

Almonds, Avocados, eggs, fish, walnuts, cheese, extra virgin olive oil.

VEGETABLES AND FRUIT:

Eat a variety of different fruits and vegetables. These supply the body with minerals and vitamins.

Some fruits and veggies contain various levels of carbohydrates, so choosing the correct ones in the right amounts means you can enjoy the healthy benefits of these tasty foods without too many carbohydrates.

Leafy green veggies are vital for nutrition as they contain high levels of antioxidants, which reduces cell damage. The darker the green, the healthier they are for you.

Find the fruits that you like! There's such a wide variety of fruits on the market. Try out something new; you might find you like it.

The more colorful your plate, the more diverse the vitamins.

(Fruit and vegetables, in general, are healthy low-fat foods, but they don't provide us with all the nutrients we need to be healthy).

SNACKS

Snacks help to keep blood sugar levels balanced throughout the day, which manages hunger. Preferably, your snacks should be high in complex carbohydrates. (Complex carbohydrates take longer to break down and provide long-lasting energy compared to simple carbohydrates like sugars. These are found in grains, beans, or fruits, especially high-fiber fruits). Try to avoid fruit juices, as they have more concentrated sugar, which could lead to inappropriate weight gain.

Types of snacks for your meal plan:

Fruit, muesli bar, chocolate bar, dried fruit and nuts, a biscuit, cheese, and crackers.

INCLUDE WATER

You may be unaware, but with bulimia, you're more than likely to be living in a state of chronic dehydration, as purging forces many of the fluids out of the body.

Water makes up approximately 60-70% of our body mass and about 80% of our brain. So even if you're slightly dehydrated, this can have a significant impact, including:

- Poor concentration
- Headaches
- Digestive disorders
- It's the number one cause for daytime fatigue

And the list continues...

Many of my bulimic clients tend to drink a lot of caffeine through coffee, tea, and diet drinks. These are all diuretics. So, it's time to cut back on these. Focus on the excellent benefits of water.

Start to introduce drinking a small amount of water regularly during the day; then, build gradually, whether you're thirsty or not. However, it's essential to avoid water at mealtimes to avoid feeling over full.

Please see step 6, for the advantages and vast benefits that drinking water provides for you.

HOW MUCH SHOULD I BE EATING?

The best nutrition guide in town is going to be your own body, especially not some fantastic new diet you've just seen. It's inside you.

Your body will let you know when you've had sufficient food. It will change from day to day, depending on how much you're moving your body. Although I don't like my clients to focus on calories, the chart below helps you determine your optimal daily calories. You may be surprised at how much your body needs.

	MODERATELY ACTIVE	ACTIVE
	30-60 min/day	60 min+/day
FEMALES - AGE		
19-30	2,200	2,400
31-50	2,000	2,200
51+	1,800	2,200
MALES - AGE		
19-30	2,800	3,000
31-50	2,600	3,000
51+	2,400	2,800

MOVING ON TO YOUR STRUCTURED EATING PROGRAM

Now you have an idea of all the exciting healthy nutrients to include in your structured eating program. Let's move on to a structured eating program example.

 But firstly keep reminding yourself, "Any weight you may or may not gain will fall off naturally as your body balances out and your powerful metabolism speeds up."

Bulimia Recovery Structured Meal Program Example:

Here's an example of a simple food plan, including the times to eat. It's a rough guide, so feel free to change the times and substitute the foods to your likings.

Eat at the same time each day, every two and a half to three hours, and stick to a strict schedule.

7:30 am
Lemon water

8:00 am (Breakfast)
Banana
½ cup or one serving cereal
1 cup milk (dairy, soy, almond, etc.)

10:30 am (Snack)
Biscuit - a hobnob is always a good choice
Granola Bar
Fruit

A handful of nuts/seed/dried fruit
Water or another drink with vitamins/ nutrients/ potassium

1:00pm (Lunch)
Turkey/chicken/egg salad/tuna sandwich on 2 slices whole wheat bread
Vegetables (Carrots, celery/tomatoes/lettuce)
Sauce (Butter/mayonnaise/ketchup/mustard)
Salad (Bean/Potato/Quinoa etc)
Dried fruits or nuts/seeds. Handful

3:00pm (Snack)
1/2 Biscuits
1 serving crackers, pretzels or popcorn
Granola bar/ handful of dried fruits
Water or another drink with vitamins/ nutrients/ potassium

6:00pm (Dinner)
Cooked protein (Grilled chicken breast/fish/other meat) (2/3 cups)
Cooked vegetables (broccoli/spinach/peas) (1/4 plate)
Cooked Starch (1 cup noodles/sweet potato/rice/bread)
Dessert: Fruit/handful of nuts/seeds

8:30 pm
1 cup yogurt /1 medium apple
Popcorn
Muffin/snack/cake/biscuit
Water or another drink with vitamins/ nutrients/ potassium

Let's talk about portion sizes for your eating plan.

At the beginning of your recovery, it's a good idea to measure or weigh out the foods so you can correctly learn what a portion size is.

To keep measuring and weighing food can be a pain in the ass. So, an offhand rule of thumb to gauge the sizes is:

Using your hand, make a fist = 1 cup or 8 oz. An example would be one cup of cereal, vegetables, fruit, rice, or pasta. (This would also equate to the size of a baseball or tennis ball).

The palm of your hand—3 oz serving of red meat, fish, or poultry.
Thumb tip = 1 teaspoon
3 x thumb tips = 1 tablespoon
1 handful of small foods like nuts = 1 oz
2 handfuls of crisps = 1 oz

NOW IT'S TIME TO CREATE YOUR NEW STRUCTURED EATING PROGRAM

Having read how to create your structured eating program, now is the time to create your own.

Complete the STRUCTURED EATING PROGRAM table in Step 4, in your workbook. Otherwise, grab your notebook and start to list what foods you're going to include in your program and follow the bulimia recovery meal example. Then make up your own recovery meal plan.

If your food program doesn't look perfect, who cares; it's you taking control and beginning with your first small nibble of breaking free from bulimia.

It's essential in the beginning to take it easy. Don't eat foods that you know are going to cause you to fall back into that old pattern.

In time, you can build up to those foods. But remember, we are focused on a healthy eating program, and junk foods don't need to be included in any healthy food program!

Keep reminding yourself:

- While you're eating regular meals and snacks, think of all the powerful positive changes your body will be making to break free from your triggers and urges to binge.

- Any weight you may gain will fall off naturally as your body balances out and your powerful metabolism speeds up.

- Your structured eating program is only temporary to get you back on track.

ASK FOR SUPPORT

One great idea to help you with your structured eating program is to have someone there to support you, such as a loved one or a friend you can trust. Having that support can be incredibly beneficial in your recovery.

It's important to give guidance on how they can help you, what you want them to do. Do you want them to eat food with you or distract you as you eat? Think about this beforehand, so you have all the help and support you need.

Be kind; oh yes, it's time to **be kind to yourself!**

What you are going to do here by beginning to introduce healthy foods is incredibly brave. Even if that leprechaun is screaming at you, your strength, learning, and courage will be extremely powerful.

It's normal to feel scared, so you must be kind and compassionate with yourself. If you do slip up, that's okay. Beating yourself up isn't going to help in your recovery process.

You're learning to overcome an illness, so you must be kind to yourself. Maybe, now is the time to forgive yourself for all the years of bingeing and purging.

HOW ARE YOU FEELING NOW?

 You may be thinking right now; *I don't think I can start eating healthily on my structured eating program.* Let me remind you, it all comes back to your thoughts about eating. It's not actually about eating the food. It's those dreaded thoughts again that can bring on feelings of fear and anxiety. BUT, and this is a big BUT... it's your choice if you listen to your thoughts, which are often incorrect! Or, you can decide here and now that it's time to start to take control!

I know it may not sound so easy, as it certainly didn't with me. My first thought was that if I were going to eat that amount of food each day, then I'd end up the size of an elephant. I'm pleased to say I never ended up with a wrinkly trunk! But more on the panic of putting weight on in Step 6.

But this is so important, AND if I could do it without any techniques to help me, then so can YOU by learning the different techniques in this book.

Before you begin:

- Zip back to Step 1 and focus on the technique "A picture of a new you." With your phrase, "I am taking positive steps toward learning how to eat healthily," step into this now. See and feel all the positive, empowering feelings. You're looking through your own eyes, absorbing all the positivity of how you're going to break free from bulimia.
- Then fire up your motivation with the "Electrify your motivation" technique from Step 2.

REMEMBER: Any weight you may gain will fall off naturally as your body balances out and your powerful metabolism speeds up.

"YOU WON'T CHANGE YOUR LIFE UNTIL YOU CHANGE SOMETHING YOU DO DAILY"

INTUITIVE EATING

Now that you've begun your structured eating program, it's time to examine how you can start to learn about your mind and body by looking at the foundations of intuitive eating and how it's going to help you in your recovery process.

The main keys are:

- Let go of any thoughts of dieting and restricting your food completely.
- Tune into your hunger and learn only to eat when you're hungry.
- Enjoy what you're eating, eating slowly, focusing on all the fabulous flavors and tastes.

- Tune in to the satisfied feeling, knowing you now have had enough food.
- Let go of food anxieties and begin to make peace with food.

"FOCUS ON HOW FAR YOU'VE COME, NOT HOW FAR YOU HAVE TO GO"

WHY DO I NEED TO EAT INTUITIVELY?

 One of the enormous critical elements for learning to eat intuitively is you cannot begin to break from the chains of bulimia if you're depriving yourself physically, mentally, or emotionally of foods, (Here I go again!). But it's the real glistening key to your recovery.

If there's any form of restriction, your body will slip back into its natural pattern of trying to survive. Your brain will automatically fall back and use that old neural pathway of driving you to binge and purge.

BACK TO BASICS

Intuitive eating is all about getting back to the basics of eating. Learning how much food your body needs for the amount of movement it's doing.

As a young child, leaving food on your plate would infuriate your parents, who would scold, "Think of all the poor starving children in the world." But, unconsciously, you were tuning into whether or not you were hungry, knowing you had enough. This natural tuning into your body is something we were all born with; it doesn't leave you. Biologically, it's inside you, maybe lurking behind a spleen, but it's there.

As a teenager, you become aware of dieting. Let's face it; diets are mentioned everywhere in magazines, adverts, on TV. Then there's the internet; oh my, what nonsense diets are there! Beware, I'm sure there's probably one skulking behind your couch! They're everywhere.

Due to dieting and restricting your food intake, this sensation of when and how much food your body needs has become buried or even super-glued behind your spleen.

But as you begin to follow your structured eating program, over time, your natural sensation of hunger and when you've had sufficient food will slowly make itself known to you.

A rosebud may be shaded by a tree, but as the sun gradually moves and shines down on the bud, it flourishes into a fabulous shimmering beauty of a flower. So may the light of understanding guide you forward in helping you in your steps to achieving your ultimate goal of "completely eating like a normal person forever more."

 Once you start to eat and feed your body the foods it requires regularly, you can then begin to tune into that sensation of hunger. And, gradually, it will hop out from behind that spleen and welcome the attention. It will guide you in your positive steps to learn how to eat again.

WILL I LOSE CONTROL?

The answer is **NO; YOU WILL STAY IN CONTROL**

Often my client's concern is if they allow themselves to begin eating again, they'll lose control and won't stop eating, which could then lead to a binge.

So, let me explain why you won't lose control. If you're depriving yourself of food (Woops! It just fell out), your mind just continually thinks about food. But as you allow yourself to start to eat again, your mind will let go and stop thinking about food all the time. That urge and need to carry on eating disappears as you start to listen to what your body is telling you by:

Becoming aware of the feeling of hunger, eating slowly, tuning in to the sense of "knowing" you've had enough, which I'll explain later in this step.

HOW DO I EAT INTUITIVELY?

ITS ALL ABOUT NUGGETS AND THEY ARE NOT CHICKEN!

There are three golden nuggets to help you in your understanding of breaking free from the chains of bulimia. This is how you're going to eat intuitively, golden nugget by golden nugget...

YOUR FIRST GOLDEN NUGGET IS: ONLY EAT WHEN YOU ARE HUNGRY

Retraining your mind and body to start eating only when hungry, rather than anxious, stressed, tired, or unhappy.

SO HOW DOES HUNGER FEEL IN THE BODY?

As a physical sensation, hunger is like an internal itch you can't scratch. The only way to satisfy it is by ingesting food. Or it's like being thirsty, which we all know how that feels. It's similar to thirst but in the stomach in a solid form.

My clients have described this in many different ways:

For most, it begins with is a physical feeling:

A grumbling sensation in the stomach. Followed by a burning sensation.

A powerful and loud emptiness, and the more you ignore your hunger, the bigger the emptiness feelings grow.

If you don't eat, you become irritable. Everything becomes annoying, and you may start to feel physically weak. Have reduced awareness. Even shaky.

If you do get to this point, then your body is going wild. Desperate for food, it will stuff any greasy carbohydrate foods you can find. So, it's crucial not to get to this stage.

THE HUNGER SCALE

The hunger scale is an excellent guide to help you to learn and understand further how much food your body needs. Your relationship with food will develop as you begin to learn how hungry you are.

The hunger scale is a scale from 1 to 10.

- 1 being when you're completely empty of food and ready to eat anything that comes into view.
- 10 is when you're stuffed.

In the past, there will have been an exploding pot of reasons why you reached out for food. But there's only one reason to eat: you're hungry!

Learning how to use the hunger scale will give you a powerful indicator of how hungry you really are.

If you didn't use the hunger scale, you could end up eating more than you need because you aren't aware of how much food you need.

HOW TO USE THE HUNGER SCALE

- Ask yourself before you eat, "how hungry am I on a scale from 1 to 10.
- If you register between 4/5/6, then you are more than likely hungry, so it's time to gobble.
- If you register 1/2/3 on the scale, then you are going to be way too hungry, this is a time for caution. As you learn how to use the hunger scale, you'll find it easier to gauge where you are and not allow yourself to get down this low. It's a danger zone, so take your eating slowly.
- If you register 7 or above, you are probably not hungry, so ask yourself, "I know I am not hungry for this food. What feelings am I trying to change?"

THE HUNGER SCALE

Ask yourself before you eat...
"How hungry am I on a scale of 1 to 10?"

1	Feeling faint & obsessed with thoughts of food	If you score 1, 2 or 3 you exhibit extreme hunger. When you eat at this level, take it slowly.
2	Famished, extremely irritable	
3	Grumbling stomach. Your mouth waters at the mere thought of food	
4	} Where you want to be	If you register 4, 5 or 6, you're probably quite hungry, so it's time to eat.
5		
6		
7	Satisfied & content fullness	If you register 7 or above, you are more than likely not hungry. Ask yourself: "I know I am not hungry for this food, what feelings am I trying to change?
8	Slightly too full	
9	Feeling heavy & uncomfortable	
10	Ready to explode!	

Print out the scale and stick this up somewhere visible for you to learn. You need to create a new positive habit of tuning into the hunger scale every time you eat to make this more conscious for you as you tune in and begin to learn about your hunger correctly.

YOUR SECOND GOLDEN NUGGET IS: AWARENESS EATING

This golden nugget is about eating slowly, intuitively, deliberately, and intentionally. Learn that it's okay to be aware of all the fabulous smells, tastes, and flavors. Over time, you can begin to enjoy the experience of eating again.

Most bulimics will wolf down their food without becoming aware of what they're actually eating. I would eat so fast, I resembled a grey wolf inhaling a mountain goat, without even taking a moment to enjoy each morsel, not even a muddy hoof.

For you, with your positive new habits and patterns, this nugget is critical because if you eat like a wolf, you won't feel the signs that you've had enough food.

As you eat, your body releases various chemicals to tell you that you're almost full, which can take up to 20 minutes, so if you continue eating without these chemical messages, your stomach becomes overstuffed. We know where that can lead you!

TOP TIPS ON SLOWING YOUR EATING DOWN?

- It's essential to have a calm, relaxed environment while you eat. Take time to eat slowly, leisurely enjoying the experience. Imagine now achieving this, feeling calm, relaxed, and happy as you eat. What a breakthrough this will be for you, and the immense achievement you'll feel. Purposefully spend at least 20 minutes eating your evening meal.
- Chew your food slowly. Why? Because digestion starts in the mouth. Saliva contains the enzyme amylase, which

helps to break down the food. If the food doesn't stay in your mouth long enough, it won't absorb this enzyme, which breaks down carbohydrates. Only a small amount of carbohydrate digestion occurs in the stomach. Therefore, the stomach will have to work harder.

- Studies recommend chewing each mouthful 32 times, although that can be tricky if you are eating jelly! If you aren't chewing your food enough, your digestive system becomes baffled. It may not produce the correct amount of enzymes needed to break down the foods eaten. With this could well come problems like bloating, diarrhea, irritability, heartburn, and many more.

- Rather than counting the number of times you are chewing your food, take your time, putting your knife and fork, sandwich, or whatever you're eating down between bites.

- Regularly stop and tune into how your stomach is feeling— checking if you are nearing the almost full sensation in the stomach, so you don't overeat.

The key here's to begin to enjoy the experience of all the fabulous flavors and tastes in what you eat.

THIRD GOLDEN NUGGET IS: TO TUNE INTO THE SATISFIED FEELINGS OF KNOWING YOU HAVE HAD ENOUGH FOOD NOW

The third golden nugget to learning to be in control of how much you eat, tuning in to how your stomach feels as you eat slowly, then start to become aware of feelings of comfortableness or a satisfying feeling in your stomach or head.

Stop eating when you have this comfortable feeling or when you're 80% full.

What's so important here is that you aren't going to be stuffing your-self, like an overfull bulging suitcase. You're going to focus on what you're eating, stop and check for signs of almost full or satisfied feel-ing, and stop eating.

It's time to leap in and meet Leptin

Leptin is a hormone in the body that sends a message to your brain to tell you that you've had enough food, which you may not be so aware of yet.

As you build on your new eating pattern and skills, you will, as you eat, get to a comfortable or satisfying stage in your stomach. This is when leptin comes in. It has leapt into your brain to tell you that you've had enough food! The more you can gradually become aware of this, the more you'll naturally have control over how much food your body needs.

Your satisfied feeling will gradually become more evident each time you eat. Before you know it, your satisfied feeling will have leapt in!

My clients have described this in so many different ways. Now is your time to learn what this sensation feels like for you.

It could be:

- A thought or a knowing such as "I've had enough," "I'm satisfied," or "I'm feeling comfortable now."
- A picture in your mind of your stomach 80% full or you, looking satisfied or comfortable, knowing you have had enough food but not stuffed.
- A comfortable, contented, or satisfied feeling.

- A physical feeling such as your stomach slightly expanding or a slight flutter in your stomach.

Trust; it's time to begin trusting yourself and your own body's natural instincts.

It's about learning about your body. If, after twenty minutes of finishing your food, you still haven't found the satisfying feeling and you're still physically hungry, have a little more food. Remember, you're learning new positive patterns and are not supposed to be starving yourself.

HOW DOES INTUITIVE EATING HELP TO STOP YOU FROM OVEREATING?

 Once your body is no longer deprived of food, and you give yourself full permission to eat when you're hungry, you'll experience freedom from bingeing and feeling crazy when you're in the same room as food. The excitement and urgency about seeking food dissipates.

You may feel terrified or anxious right now. But once you start to eat intuitively, you'll begin to free yourself of your past habits and patterns. The obsessive negative thoughts around food will loosen and the fears and struggles you once had with bulimia will eventually disappear.

By using this method of gauging how hungry you are, eating slowly, and then tuning into your satisfied feeling of fullness, you'll be in control. You'll be as happy as the cat that swallowed the canary!

HOW DO I KNOW IF I AM READY TO BEGIN TO IMPLEMENT INTUITIVE EATING?

You can begin eating intuitively at any time during your recovery. However, if you're underweight and malnourished, your signals of hunger and fullness are confused, so you need to focus on beginning to eat again with your structured eating program and learn first to loosen the hold on the triggers, urges, bingeing, and purging.

Once you're feeling confident with your structured eating program and have started to include the fearful foods we'll be discussing next, which is usually eight weeks or so from starting, it's then time to begin intuitive eating. Once you're ready, start implementing your intuitive eating.

YOU'VE GOT THIS...

By taking control, anxiety and fears will subside as you learn to make peace with food. The obsessive and negative thoughts about food and your body lessen. What emerges is a considerable amount of space for many wonderful things, like more pleasant thoughts and actions that come in to replace all the negativity that has been bubbling in your cauldron.

"THE SECRET TO SUCCESS...IS FOUND IN YOUR DAILY ROUTINE"

FORBIDDEN FOODS

IT IS TIME TO FEEL THE FEAR AND EAT IT ANYWAY!

WHAT IS ON THE OTHER SIDE OF YOUR FEAR?

I want to discuss how important it is for your recovery to begin to turn toward foods that you've labeled bad/fearful foods, forbidden foods, foods that you think caused you to binge, your trigger foods.

But it's not the bad food that has brought on your negative feelings about the food; it's your destructive thoughts about having bad foods. It's that toxic evil leprechaun roaring!

In the beginning, many of my clients, because of their anxiety, tell themselves that they'll face these foods when that devious leprechaun calms down. However, only when you expose yourself to these foods will the anxiety begin to lessen, and you'll feel less afraid, less fearful of these foods.

WHEN SHOULD I START TO IMPLEMENT MY FEARFUL FOODS?

Just the thought of this may be incredibly daunting, making you scared or panicky even, and you might be thinking, "Where on earth would I start?" This is an excellent question. The answer is when you've started to follow your eating program and feel more confident, you can begin to address your forbidden foods.

Although for some of my clients, they like to dive right in and take the bull by the horns and immediately start to eat their fearful foods within their structured eating program.

Everyone is different, so it's essential to do what feels right for you.

IT'S TIME TO PUT ONE FOOT OR JUST A TOE OR EVEN JUST THE TOENAIL OUTSIDE OF YOUR COMFORT ZONE!

Your evil leprechaun is wailing. I'm not saying it's going to be easy to eat forbidden foods. But it's time to start thinking differently and challenge yourself, toenail by toenail.

When you start to introduce these foods into your eating program, you'll feel a massive shift. That once fearful, anxious hold these foods had over you will begin to loosen and disperse. They'll no longer have that hold over you, and you'll be free to eat whatever you want. How wonderful will that be?

I want you now to make a list of your bad/fearful foods, starting with the least challenging up to the most challenging. As you work through the list, over time, eating each fearful food at least five times. If it still makes you fearful, then take your time and eat it again until you feel calmer about eating it. Do this as many times as you need to. Then, move onto the next fearful food on your list until you've worked through them all. Once completed, start to introduce them into your eating program.

 Complete the FEARFUL FOODS table in Step 4, in your workbook. Otherwise, grab your notebook and create your list below.

FEARFUL FOODS

SCALE	FOOD	LEPRECHAUN'S THOUGHTS	YOUR HEALTHY POSITIVE VOICE IS TELLING YOU.
(10 = MOST FEARFUL)			

As you do this, give yourself positive motivational phrases of encouragement.

 For example: "I'm learning to eat this food, and as I do so, I feel calm and relaxed."

ASK FOR SUPPORT

Similar to your structured eating program, what will help you with this toenail dipping is to have someone there to support you. And be gentle with yourself! What you're going to do here by facing your fear foods is incredibly brave.

It's normal to feel scared and out of control; the fact that you're even thinking about dipping your toenail in is a brave step forward. Stay focused because you can change how you feel about your forbidden foods.

Wow, you've taken huge positive strides toward breaking all your bulimia patterns by beginning to introduce your structured eating program. I'm so proud of you, as I know this may feel scary and uncomfortable for you, but you can do this, one little step at a time.

To empower you to stay focused, when you're ready, ask for help and support from a loved one or a friend.

DEMI LOVATO (American singer/actress) has remained vocal about her ongoing struggle with food.

Demi was speaking about her battle with bulimia, saying, "Recovery is possible." After many years of struggling with bulimia, she also stated, "I'm not going to sacrifice my mental health to have the perfect body."

So, before we jump into Step 5 and learn to reprogram your mind to break free from bulimia, let's look at the action steps you've acquired here:

STEP 4 - HERE ARE YOUR KEY EMPOWERING ACTION STEPS:

- Create your structured eating program introducing healthy, balanced, energizing foods for you to start to enjoy.
- Keep reminding yourself any weight you may gain will fall off naturally as your body balances out, and your robust metabolism speeds up.
- PLUS, THE 3 Rs:
  - Your cravings will begin to Reduce.
  - Your urges will begin to Reduce
  - Your binges will begin to Reduce.
- Begin to turn toward foods that you've labeled fearful foods and begin to introduce them into your structured eating program, but only when you're ready!
- Again, when you're feeling confident about your structured eating program, begin to introduce your intuitive eating plan, your genuine golden nuggets of how you're going to take control, once and for all, of how much food your body needs.

- Be kind to yourself; you deserve it. Take this all very slowly. If you slip off your pathway to freedom, that's okay. What can you learn from it? Then hop back onto your pathway; you'll be further along on this path, having learned from your slip.

Remember to keep using the "Electrifying your Motivation" technique when that leprechaun wakes up and starts whispering, "You don't deserve your freedom" or "You can't do this." Because You ABSOLUTELY CAN, and you're taking back control of your life.

It may not be easy at times, but you deserve a happy life. You'll move forward toward this with all your new learnings so far, making that decisive breakthrough you've only dreamt of in the past. Now you're taking action; you have an exciting future waiting for you.

STEP 5

HOW CAN I GET OUT
OF THIS DARK HOLE?

**"IF YOU FIND YOURSELF IN A DARK HOLE,
THE FIRST THING YOU DO IS STOP DIGGING & THEN
BEGIN TO LEARN HOW TO START LIVING"**

Wahoooo! It's time to reprogram your mind.

Your empowering learnings from Step 4:

- First, let's just recap what you've learned in Step 4. Having started with your structured eating program, you're now moving forward and taking back control of your life, which is an incredibly powerful huge stride toward your end goal. And if you've started to learn to be somewhat confident, eating your forbidden foods, fantastic; it's a hugely exciting change. If not, you'll know when you're ready.
- Whether or not you've begun your intuitive eating program, these are such powerful steps toward that new you. I'm so proud of you, and I hope you are too!
- Let's get motivated to move on to Step 5. Imagine how you're going to be in the future free from bulimia forever!

Using your motivational anchor, pressing your finger and thumb together, genuinely feel that inspiration and motivating force; allow it to wash over your whole body now.

The positive guidance you'll be learning here in Step 5:

- You'll be learning how powerful your incredibly creative imagination is compared to your willpower and how you can reprogram your mind to change your negative habits and behaviors.
- You'll be learning about your beliefs and how to change your limiting beliefs instantly. With a super powerful technique called "Change your beliefs instantly."
- Understanding how stress affects your everyday life. As it's your interpretation of an event that then triggers your stress and by tuning into your stress, you can learn to react more positively to it.
- Also, you'll be shown a technique called "Thought Stopping." As now you are more aware of your own evil leprechaun and his debilitating whisperings, this technique is fantastic to stop him in his tracks and change your thinking.

Stay focused ... Here we gooooo.

IMAGINATION VS. WILL POWER

Is your willpower working right now?

In the past, how often have you genuinely tried to stop that urge that leads to your binge, but no matter what you do, you just can't stop yourself?

And then in swoops those evil thoughts, *I just can't control myself. It's all my fault; if only I had more willpower.*

Ummmm, if this is the case, then your willpower is probably not working so well.

SO, WHAT IS WILLPOWER?

It's your drive, determination, or self-control to resist temptation in order to achieve a long-term goal. It's a strength we see in other people and want for ourselves.

To be Frank, whoever Frank is, you didn't just decide you wanted bulimia. You had no control as the patterns developed. Therefore, using willpower to address all the links patterns and triggers isn't going to work.

Willpower is about self-control. For me, even though my bulimia seemed to be the only thing in my life I could control, I had no control over any part of my thinking, feelings, bingeing, or purging. It just happened. I was so confused. There was no willpower; it had left the room!

Now, you may be thinking, *without willpower, how am I ever going to break free from bulimia?*

But let me explain; scientific research has shown it's almost impossible to break any habit only using your willpower. You need to reprogram your mind too.

Your imagination is so much more powerful than any willpower you may have right now.

"IMAGINATION WILL OFTEN CARRY US TO WORLDS THAT NEVER WERE. BUT WITHOUT IT, WE GO NOWHERE" —CARL SAGAN

WHAT IS YOUR IMAGINATION?

Your imagination is your ability to form pictures or ideas in your mind of things that you haven't experienced.

As you've learned, we all have images that run through our minds continuously, whether we're aware of them or not. Your imagination is now creating images in your head to help maintain these negative behaviors, patterns, and triggers. So, what we need to do is turn this around and have your imagination help you break these patterns and focus on new empowering behaviors.

LET'S TEST YOUR IMAGINATION

Imagine a large bar of your favorite chocolate or food in front of you.

Study that chocolate bar, then tell yourself with all your willpower that you aren't going to eat it. Now imagine the taste of that chocolate melting on your tongue, the pure, smooth, creamy texture. How is that making you feel now? Do you really want to eat it? Oh, yes, I'm sure you do.

Next, imagine you're at the hairdresser, and that chocolate bar is in front of you but covered in slugs and their slime trail. You've just had your hair cut, and the hair has fallen onto the slime. Does it still seem as delicious now? Probably not! Yuk.

See how powerful your imagination is.

HOW MANY?

With 60,000 to 70,000 thoughts that run through our minds each day, 95% of them are the same thoughts we had yesterday!

So, if we're having the same thoughts as we had yesterday, what happens:

- That creates the same behaviors.
- The same behaviors will always create the same experiences.
- Then, the same experiences will always create the same thoughts and feelings.

If you have less than 5% new thoughts, how are you going to stop this pattern?

 The answer lies within you by adjusting your behaviors, habits, and patterns, and one way you can do this is by using your imagination.

This slug-infested chocolate experience shows you how powerful your mind is, how your mind can change everything. Your thoughts are the driver, and your habits can sabotage your plans to stay free from bingeing tomorrow.

We are all indeed creatures of our habits. So, it's not surprising that we fail.

"IF YOU CONTINUE TO THINK THE WAY YOU THOUGHT YOU WILL NEVER BREAK FREE AND YOU WILL END UP DISTRAUGHT" —KATE HUDSON-HALL & WAYNE PURDIN

NOW IS THE TIME TO REPROGRAM YOUR THINKING

What I'm suggesting is that you begin to change the way you think using your imagination.

For example, if you were to think about how your life would be completely free from bulimia, what you would look like, feel, say to yourself? What happens is your unconscious mind will begin to develop and focus on that imaginary reality. It will slowly evolve into physical reality and into your life constructively.

Your unconscious mind is so unbelievably ingenious and compelling, and right now, you aren't using it correctly, with the way you're thinking.

YOUR NEGATIVE THINKING

If you are thinking to yourself, *I am fat today; I can't control my need to be thin,*

what happens? Your unconscious mind will be focused on what it's being told. With this sort of negative thinking, you're helping your unconscious mind to focus on your weight or food, which is exactly where you need to steer clear of.

For example, if you think to yourself, *I must stop making myself sick,* you'll immediately create an image in your head. It will be a flash of a picture of you making yourself sick. Then that will reinforce the fact that you'll go ahead into that downward spiral of the binge cycle.

If you continue to believe what you tell yourself, you'll never be free from bulimia. It's your choice if you continue to choose to listen to what you tell yourself. OR you can choose to change and STOP listening to all this negativity. This is where your imagination will help you do this.

HOW DO YOU REPLACE YOUR NEGATIVE THINKING WITH POSITIVE THINKING?

 Scientific research has shown that visualization techniques significantly improve our ability to change positively by replacing old negative images with positive images. You can begin to change the way you feel, how amazing would that be?

In addition to positive images in the brain, you also want to create positive emotions to support those new images. The feelings can be guided by what you feed your mind; you have the power to change your beliefs and behavior.

This is one of the reasons why it's incredibly important to keep stepping into that new you method using the "The New You" technique to empowering yourself in Step 1.

**"WHAT THE MIND CAN CONCEIVE AND BELIEVE,
THE MIND CAN ACHIEVE" —NAPOLEON HILL**

BELIEFS

What is a belief?

A belief is the confidence you have about what something means. Your beliefs create maps that guide you toward the good or bad you have in our life. They come from past experiences, whether they were a painful or enjoyable experience.

What is a limiting belief?

Your limiting belief is something you believe to be true about yourself, someone else, or the world that limits you in some way. These beliefs hold you back from moving forward, keeping you stuck, focusing on the negative aspects of your behavior.

The challenge with limiting beliefs is that you may not even be aware that you have any. But unfortunately, they'll be there, lurking in the depths of your teapot somewhere, waiting to spring out of the spout!

For example:

Perhaps you decide you're going to stop bingeing and purging. You stick to this for a few hours or even a day. But then temptation gets the better of you.

Thinking to yourself, *Arrrr, I need to binge; I'm hopeless.* You then resist any temptation until you eventually come to the limiting belief, *I just can't stop bingeing and purging, I'm a failure.* Then, as this pattern continues, the belief you're a failure develops over time and will continue to build if not addressed.

Or how often have you heard yourself say such things as "I have no control over my eating" or "I'm hopeless" or "I'm stupid"? These are all examples of limiting beliefs that are holding you back from moving forward positively.

A limiting belief is a thought you have about yourself that you believe is true due to past negative experiences. But, and this is a big BUT... they actually aren't true; they're a load of twaddle!

As Tony Robbins says:

"What we can or cannot do, what we consider possible or impossible, is rarely a function of our true capability. It is more likely a function of our beliefs about who we are."

Where do beliefs come from? How are they formed?

We create our beliefs through our experiences or by accepting what others tell us is true. Most of our core beliefs are created when we're young children.

When we're born, we have a clean slate without any predetermined beliefs, but as we go through life, the beliefs build. When we're young, we're like a sponge, absorbing our environment, and all around us, we're unable to differentiate between what the truth is and what is false. Often, we accept what we're told as the truth.

Our parents play a big part in moulding our beliefs, and then we're off to school, which also plays an essential role in the creation of our beliefs.

As I mentioned earlier in my memoir, my limiting belief that "I was stupid," which started from the age of five, was continually being told to me, and I started to believe it to be accurate and to treat it as a fact. As I got older, my limiting belief began to flourish into an acorn. Then, as I became an adult with different experiences throughout my life, before I knew it, I had a stunning oak tree sprouting from every orifice!

"DON'T JUST GO THROUGH LIFE; IT'S NOW TIME TO GROW INTO YOUR LIFE. BECOME THE SEED THAT FLOURISHES"

Your limiting beliefs then begin to control any decisions you make in your life, until your awareness steps in and you become aware of the negative behaviors and decide to change them.

YOUR RESOURCES ARE WAITING TO HOP OUT AND HELP YOU CHANGE

You already have the resources you need to change. You may not believe this, but you do.

For me, when I finally understood that my limiting belief, "I was stupid," wasn't actually true, I had a choice to either continue to believe this and think in this way for the next 109 years or to change and review my thinking.

I learned how to create a new positive belief to counteract that old belief I was stupid. For example, "I can learn to do better in my course." Specific but straightforward is the key. This new belief could well have some evidence at the end of it all if I stayed focused on what I truly wanted.

What are your limiting beliefs?

It's time to replace your old, disempowering beliefs with new empowering beliefs, but first, you need to identify what your old beliefs are.

As I mentioned, you have many limiting beliefs about yourself, but we want to focus on the limiting beliefs that are going to have the most significant impact first; then you can go on and deal with the others.

Key elements for your new belief:

- It has to be simple and specific.
- It has to address the old belief.
- It has to be opened and revisable.

 Complete YOUR OLD/NEW LIMITING BELIEFS table in Step 5, in your workbook. Otherwise, grab your notebook and looking through the example list below, make a list of all your limiting beliefs. Once you've identified your old beliefs, then look through the list of new beliefs in the table and begin to create new beliefs to focus on instead.

OLD BELIEF	NEW BELIEF
"People who are thin are pretty."	"I can be happy however I look."
"I must be perfect and not make mistakes."	"It's okay to make some mistakes."
"I'm not good enough."	"I am good enough to live a free and happy life."
"I am worthless; I am not worthy of living	"I am worthy of living my life free from bulimia."
without bulimia."	"I am learning to be in total control of the foods I eat."
"I have no control over my eating."	"I am taking steps to believe I am lovable."
"If I am fat, I'll be unlovable."	"I am loveable."

"BELIEVE YOU CAN, AND YOU ARE HALFWAY THERE" —THEODORE ROOSEVELT

Here we go, time to create your new empowering belief with the "Change Your Beliefs Instantly Technique."

"CHANGE YOUR BELIEFS INSTANTLY" TECHNIQUE

Part One

1. Think of the negative belief that's standing in your way of breaking the cycle of bingeing and purging. For example: "I can't stop bingeing and purging; I am a failure." See, hear, and feel yourself doing this behavior and look at all the qualities of the pictures you make. Go through your list of submodalities from Step 1 and write down all the answers. For example: is it in color or black and white, moving or still, how big is the picture, is it close up or far away, clear or blurry? Work your way through the list.

2. Next, find a strong belief that you know is true, that you're sure about. For example: "The sun is going to rise tomorrow" or if you live in England… "It will rain sometime soon!" Again, using the submodalities from the list, note the submodalities of this belief. For example: "I can learn some techniques to help me control my eating."

3. Compare the two, making a note of what the differences are (e.g., size of the pictures, color or black and white, moving or still, and so on).

Part Two

Now onto the fun part, with your two lists, you're going to create your new empowering belief.

1. Think of your new empowering belief (chose from the previous list or create your own), something similar to "I am taking positive steps toward learning how to eat healthily." Now change everything about this new belief; all the submodalities from the list from your firm belief that you know

are true. Move the picture to the same position, same size, distance, colors, brightness, etc., producing the same fabulous feelings you had.

2. Now step into that new belief, looking through your own eyes and absorb all the powerful feelings of believing you can break free and live your life happy, healthy, and free from bulimia. Absorb this incredible feeling and when it begins to subside, step out of the experience.

 Fantastic! Now you can hop into your new empowering belief whenever you aren't feeling too good about yourself, do this at least five times per day, if you will, please.

Video Demonstration Link: https://bulimiasucks.com/change-your-beliefs-instantly/

> **"YOU DECIDE EVERY MOMENT OF EVERY DAY WHO YOU ARE AND WHAT YOU BELIEVE IN. YOU GET A SECOND CHANCE EVERY SECOND" —TONY ROBINS**

PLUS... ITS TIME TO BRING OUT YOUR ACTING SKILLS

What happens if you pretend your new belief is true?

Have you ever heard the great phrase "Fake it till you make it"?

Oh, yes, it's a fine saying. Just pretend or act as if you already are worthy, clever, in control of your eating, and by doing this, you're halfway there, pretending that you have control of your eating.

So, start to make your new empowering belief work for you by pretending you can already deal with your urges that your leprechaun has caused by whispering in your ear. It's time to brainwash yourself into believing you can achieve whatever you wish.

LET'S TALK ABOUT YOUR STRESSSSS

Stress can saturate all aspects of our lives with a potent mix of bodily symptoms and anxious thinking. It's time to unravel stress-inducing thoughts. See them in a more accurate perspective, and that weakens their hold.

What is stress?

There are many different stresses, including both:

External sources—social factors such as pressure for that perfect body or hurtful comments, family problems, stuck in traffic, financial issues, work demands, and the list goes on.

Internal sources—thoughts such as a negative interpretation of a situation that triggers a stress response that leads you to binge and purge.

Interpretation matters

Your stress levels are directly related to your interpretation of an event that triggers the stress. Imagine you found the biggest, ugliest toad in the garden, one person might be afraid while others may be calm and find It exciting.

No one can avoid stressful experiences; our lives are brimming with them. The goal is to manage your stress skillfully. A crucial part of this is to be aware of your internal worry, your devious leprechaun, and his thoughts and stories as they contribute to your stress.

LEARN HOW TO RESPOND RATHER THAN REACT

One quick, sure-fire way to reduce your stress is to breathe!

Let's look at how you can use your breathing positively to guide you through painful, uncomfortable, scary feelings.

First, you need to understand how your breathing works.

When you exhale slightly longer than your inhale, a signal is sent to your brain to turn up your parasympathetic nervous system and turn down your sympathetic nervous system. Let me explain.

What's the difference between the two?

Your sympathetic nervous system:

When you breathe in, you activate your sympathetic nervous system, which activates your stress hormones like cortisol that start pumping through your bloodstream.

- Heart rate increases
- Blood pressure rises
- Breathing speeds up, pupils dilate, and blood vessels constrict
- Sweat increases

You become more alert and tension increases. You're preparing your body to face a threat, which was helpful when we had to fight off that saber-toothed tiger! But if the threat is "I'm late for a meeting," this response isn't especially helpful and can be damaging. It's also called the fight or flight response. It's our anxious state.

When cortisol is high too often and for too long, it disturbs the body's hormone balance, which creates stressful feelings like anxiety.

Your parasympathetic nervous system:

When we breathe out, you activate your parasympathetic nervous system, which activates your:

- Muscles to relax
- Heart rate to drop
- Blood pressure to lower
- The breath rate to normalize

You feel more relaxed and calmer. And we want more of this!

Guiding your breathing to exhale longer than you inhale will help you to feel calmer and more relaxed. Focusing on your breathing gives you control of your responses, and, yes, you'll respond rather than react.

This breathing technique very quickly calms the physiology of the body and brain, and most people feel calmer and less anxious within two to three breaths.

So, using this technique, you'll lower stress response and improve your physical and emotional health.

"RELAXATION BREATHING" TECHNIQUE

Here's how you are going to feel calmer:

Breathe in through the nose to the count of four down into your stomach. Then breathe out through your mouth to the count of eight. When you breathe out, purse lips and gently blow like you're blowing out a candle or bubble. Repeat this two more times.

 Practice this breathing technique often throughout the day, especially whenever you're stressed, anxious, scared, or tense. To make this one of your many new habits, pick a few times during the day and set your alarm to go off at those times...AND BREATHE.

"THOUGHT STOPPING" TECHNIQUE

Another way to reduce your stress and toxic leprechaun's mutterings is with a powerful technique called "Thought Stopping."

Thought stopping is a technique for stopping and challenging that leprechaun's beastly dialog and the escalating emotional whirlwind of increasing negative feelings with a "stop" command. Giving you a sense of control, you're breaking the harmful thought habit and reinforcing a sense of reassurance.

WHY DOES IT WORK?

 Why thought stopping works is pretty straightforward; you interrupt the evil leprechaun's beastly mutterings with a "stop" command as a reminder and distraction. And it diverts your attention from damaging repetitive thought habits.

As you may or may not be aware yet, usually, your obsessive thoughts tend to repeat in your mind. Left unchecked, they become automatic in a never-ending cycle of spiraling disaster. When using the thought-stopping technique, you become aware of the damaging thought chains and redirect your attention away from harmful repetitive thought habits.

Thought stopping requires consistent motivation and doesn't work on more than one negative, stressful thought at a time.

Now you've identified more of a pattern of what happens that creates the urges from Step 3. Now you're going to learn how to stop these horrific thoughts. Here we go:

Step 1. Notice the thought

Close your eyes and imagine a situation in which a stressful thought/ feeling may occur.

Step 2. Thought Interruption

Set a timer for two minutes. Close your eyes and ponder on your stressful thought. When you hear the ring, shout, "Stop!" then "Get lost" in whatever terminology you wish!

If you're the visual type, also imagine a giant stop sign in your head.

You could also have a loose rubber band on your wrist to snap at this point. If you don't have one available, you could snap your fingers or even pinch yourself.

If you do have an evil leprechaun gripping tightly onto your shoulder, shouting his anxiety-provoking nonsense, then as you shout, "Stop," physically swipe him from your shoulder at the same time.

Now, let your mind empty of all but the calm and non-anxious thoughts and reroute your mind to an inspiring or distracting thought instead. So, rather than your obsessive thought, make up some positive statements and images that are appropriate in the target situation.

A rerouting thought might be a saying that encourages you or a memory that's empowering or relaxing.

Set a goal of about thirty seconds after the stop.

If the distressing thought returns during that time, shout, "Stop!" swiping away the evil leprechaun from your shoulder and "Get lost," snapping your rubber band or snap your fingers.

Step 3. Now do this without the timer

Now take control of the evil leprechaun's whispering without the timer. While pondering on the unwanted thought, shout, "Stop!" and "Get lost," and then bring up the giant stop sign and snap your rubber band or pinch yourself.

- When you succeed in stopping the thought on several occasions with the shouted command, begin interrupting the thought with a "Stop!" and "Get lost" in a usual voice.

- After succeeding in stopping the thought by using your normal speaking voice, start interrupting the thought with "Stop!" and "Get lost" in a whisper.
- When the whisper completely interrupts your stressful thoughts, imagine hearing "Stop!" and "Get lost" shouted inside your mind.

When you can achieve this successfully, that means that you can stop thoughts alone or in public without anyone knowing what you're doing.

You might want to write down the thoughts to help you clarify it, to challenge it, and then shred or burn it.

 Excellent! Changing your thoughts will take time, so I want you to practice thought-stopping every day as many times as possible, in fact, all day. Over time, you'll be able to stop unwanted thoughts immediately.

Video Demonstration Link: https://bulimiasucks.com/thought-stopping/

IRELAND BALDWIN

The 24-year-old daughter of Alec Baldwin and Kim Basinger opened up about her past struggles with anorexia on her Instagram Story when she shared an old photo of herself along with the caption, "Anorexia throwback." Ireland also posted a photo of her younger self posing in a bikini, writing, "Nope."

"I battled with many eating disorders and body issues as a younger girl, and it took me a long time to find self-love and acceptance!

Trust me, all that pain and destruction I inflicted on myself wasn't worth it. Turning down so. Many. Sides. Of. Fries. Wasn't worth it!!" the model wrote (Pearl, 2020).

STEP 5 - HERE ARE YOUR KEY EMPOWERING ACTION STEPS:

Having read through this step and with all your powerful learnings, you can now begin to see there's a light at the end of your tunnel. By creating the correct program in your mind, you can change your focus, start to think more positively and find it easier to separate your urges from your binges, using your strong influential image of how you want to be in the future.

- You've now learned the difference between willpower and your super creative imagination, which you can now use to reprogram your mind and open up to the self-control and determination to resist all your past temptations to binge and purge.
- You've become more aware of your limiting beliefs and the thoughts you have about yourself that you believe are accurate due to past negative experiences, and you now understand that, actually, these aren't true!
- Having listed your limiting beliefs and created new positive beliefs, you can now start your acting skills. Pretend that you can cope with situations that trigger your binge eating as you brainwash yourself into believing it.
- Stress plays a significant role in everyone's life, so as you start to address your stress, you can reassess your distress. Use your breathing to reduce your stress.
- You've tuned into your thinking and now interrupt these painful thoughts with your new skill of thought stopping.

Shouting at the voice to STOP and instructing it to "Get lost" will give you a sense of control as you work through the steps and then reroute your mind to an inspiring or distracting thought instead.

Learning all these incredible tools and techniques are giving you the power to change your story.

You aren't alone and deserve a fulfilling, happy life. By motivating yourself and staying focused, you can achieve your dream free from bulimia.

So, let's not wait. Let's move on to learning how to deal with any weight issues in Step 6.

STEP 6

I DONT WANT TO PUT ON WEIGHT, WILL THIS HAPPEN?

**"IF YOU PLANT THE SEED, THE MOTIVATION
WILL GROW" —KATE HUDSON-HALL**

Your empowering learnings from Step 5:

- Understanding the difference between your willpower and your super creative imagination, you can now use your imagination to help propel you into your positive future easier.
- You've learned about your limiting negative beliefs and how thoughts about yourself that you believe to be true due to difficult past experiences aren't true. It's your choice to listen to them or not.
- How are you progressing with the "Thought Stopping" technique? Keep shouting at the leprechaun and his evil drivel, swiping him from your shoulder again and again, and, over time, he'll become quieter until he eventually runs out of juice.

The positive guidance you'll be learning here in Step 6:

In this step, the key elements you're going to learn to help you deal with a weight increase in your recovery are:

- What will happen to your body when you stop bingeing and purging. This will help reduce some of the negative thoughts and give you tools to help you deal better with what may happen.
- If you were to gain weight, learning how you can manage this. Understanding that weight gain is only temporary. It's part of your body's healing process.
- Understanding the humungous benefits of drinking... no, not alcohol... water.
- Also, you'll be learning a powerful technique called "Spin and Win" to help you with not only these scared feelings about putting on weight but also any other painful, complicated feelings that you have about anything.

TO WEIGHT OR NOT TO WAIT? NO, START NOW...

If you are like so many, in fact, most people with bulimia, one of their leading causes for not breaking free from bulimia to live a happy life is a worry of putting weight on.

 The goal in this step is to understand that weight gain is usually _only temporary_. It won't last forever; it's your body adjusting to your new eating plan. As your body recognizes that it will be getting the right nutritious foods, your weight will adapt.

KNOWING I WILL PUT WEIGHT ON, HOW WILL THAT HELP ME?

I think it's crucial for your recovery process to have a clear under-standing of what's happening to your body, as this will:

- Help you to feel less scared about the changes.
- Reduce some of the negative thoughts chattering around in your head.
- Help you to deal better with what may happen.
- Help you to feel more positive about why you're doing this. Oh yes, we like more positivity.

Remember, your goal, as you read through this book, is to learn tools and techniques to help you to "BREAK FREE FROM BULIMIA." Temporary weight changes aren't worth chucking away your deci-sion to change now and free yourself from bulimia.

PURGE LEARNING... DO YOU KNOW HOW MUCH FOOD YOU REALLY PURGE?

Much research has been done on bulimics and their food intake, which I've found interesting and thought you would too.

This may be a surprise to you.

When bingeing and purging, a certain portion of the food will stay in your stomach and intestines.

So, whether you go on a:

Small binge (eating roughly 1,500 cal) or

Big binge (eating roughly 3,500 cal)

Your body will hold onto the same number of calories regardless, which research shows us is around 1,100 cal to 1,200 cal.

In a study at the Pittsburgh Human Feeding Laboratory, a group of bulimic women was carefully monitored as they binged and purged, while the calories were calculated.

Once they had made themselves sick, the results would be examined, and the number of calories would be calculated. (Imagine how horrific it would have been for those women?)

The researchers then calculated out the number of calories eaten to the amount purged. Here's the interesting part, the women's average consumption of calories was 2,131. Once they had vomited, they discovered they only vomited 979 calories. So, they were still retaining 46% of the calories!

So, I'm sorry to tell you, even if you are an expert in purging, you'll only be able to vomit 50-60% of the food eaten, because if you binged on 3,500 calories and then vomited, you'd still hold onto 1,750 calories.

What can we learn from this?

It's not possible to rid your body of all the foods eaten. Therefore, it certainly isn't going to help you become slimmer.

WHY WEIGHT?

From the research done over the years, bulimia isn't effective in managing your weight.

But once you've followed your eating program, and as long as you eat intuitively and exercise, you must understand that your weight will eventually stabilize!

Think about all that you've put your body through with bulimia: living on empty, with no fuel, severely dehydrated, plus, all the other struggles it has had.

As you know... here I go again... When you do start to eat fantastic nutritious food again, your body, to begin with, will go into a frenzy, until it understands that regular fuel is coming. Then it will speed up your metabolism, rehydrate you, and give you newfound energy.

As you take that first step in your eating program and the first morsel passes through your body, every single cell starts to celebrate and goes from a shriveled raisin into a flourishing rehydrated beefy grape.

WEIGHT... IT MIGHT NOT HAPPEN!

As you follow your eating program, you may or MAY NOT put weight on, but it COULD have an impact on your weight. Of course, everyone is different, although you may stay at the same weight or put on a small amount of weight.

 Did you know that dehydration is one of the top killers in people with bulimia? Therefore, as you gradually start to introduce drinking water daily, the added water in your body could increase your weight in the short term. But this is your pathway to freedom.

During your recovery, if you were to fall back into your old habit, the bingeing and purging can be a cause of weight gain. It disrupts your body. It upsets not only your positive new eating patterns but also the cycle.

"FOR EVERY REASON IT'S NOT POSSIBLE, THERE ARE HUNDREDS OF PEOPLE WHO HAVE FACED THE SAME CIRCUMSTANCES AND SUCCEEDED" —JACK CANFIELD.

WHAT ABOUT THE BULIMIA BLOAT?

 Let's discuss the dreaded bloating, as this seems to be a common problem with my clients recovering from bulimia.

As I mentioned above, it can take time for your body to change from the survival mode to a positive, healthy working body. So, a little weight could well be put on. But let me reassure you; this is okay. It's a common symptom of recovery, probably due to bloating, sometimes referred to as the "bulimia bloat" or "recovery bloat," which is a frequent pattern in recovery as your body begins to adjust and balance out.

What causes the bloating?

If you've been bingeing and purging for years, depriving yourself of healthy foods, your metabolism slows down, and your body stops digesting foods correctly. As you begin to introduce healthy foods, to begin with:

- The food will stay in your stomach longer due to the muscles in your intestinal tract becoming weakened.
- It also doesn't get broken down correctly, as the digestive enzymes and healthy bacteria are affected.
- This causes uncomfortable bloating and gas.

The good news, this won't last long; it typically occurs within the first few days and lasts for only a few weeks. Everyone is different. But it's important to remember this is your body's way of healing, and **it will stop swelling**.

You must hear that:

**Your bloating is NOT real weight gain.
It's NOT you getting fat.
It's the bulimia bloat and is TEMPORARY.
Your stomach will REDUCE.**

How will you feel physically and mentally if you do get the bulimia bloat?

1. Physically you may feel uncomfortable, your clothes and jeans may be too tight, you may have stomach pains, but it will all be worth it in the end; it's your body healing. As you eat with foods digesting in your stomach, it may feel unnatural.

2. Mentally you may go into a panic, and many negative thoughts and feelings come flooding in, as you have not only put weight on, which is terrifying, but you may also feel vulnerable, and it can be frightening. You need to remind yourself that this is only temporary and stay focused on your end goal of being free from bulimia.

What if I Slip Up?

If you do end up down that old slippery path of bingeing and purging, that's okay. Steer clear from mentally beating yourself up, which, let's be honest, you've spent a long time doing. It's time to change the way you think. Be kind to yourself; yes, you have slipped up, but so be it; learn from it what you can do differently, then move on.

Ask yourself, "What would be the first step you would take to clear your mind and bring yourself back to your goal?"

Some ideas:

- Use your new thought-stopping skills to shout down your leprechaun's wailing.
- Step into your image of "The New You" really feel what it's going to be like free from all this negativity, changing whatever you need to, to make this so empowering.
- Electrify your motivation, press your finger and thumb, really feeling that motivation exploded as you move forward.
- Maybe you've identified a shriveled old belief still hanging on in there, like "I'm such a failure." Then go back to Step 5, and begin to reprogram your mind with the "Changing your Belief Instantly" technique.
- Use your new technique of "Shrink and Blink" from step 2, to free you of the problematic thought image and feeling.

Plus, you'll be learning other techniques in this book to break your patterns, so read on.

HOW TO BEAT YOUR BLOATING BEAST

To beat this bloating beast, you have to keep eating, keep nourishing your body with adequate nutrients and sufficient calories consistently. If you don't, your body will stay in the starvation mode and grab onto and hold onto every nutrient you eat.

Ideas that can help beat that bloating beast are:

- Hang around positive, supportive people; it's so important to surround yourself with positivity, people who are going to listen if you want to talk or leave you alone if you wish to be on your own.
- You need to begin to hydrate your body by drinking water regularly throughout the day. It will help with the bloating and will also:

1. Improve your kidney function, allowing excess water and sodium to be flushed out of the system.
2. It will allow all the fabulous nutrients and waste to flow in and out of the cells and help to repair damaged cells. (More on the benefits of water later in this step).
   - I advise my clients to wear loose, comfortable clothing while your body heals; wearing tight clothes can feel uncomfortable and has been known to trigger negative thoughts and feelings, which is the last thing we want.
   - Take gentle exercise, maybe going for a slow walk, not power walking, to begin with, please. It's a known fact that exercise helps to speed up the metabolism and move the food through your stomach and digestive tract but take the advice of your doctor.

- Mirror mirror on the wall, it's time to avoid them once and for all! I would recommend you skip past those mirrors without a glance; to keep studying your body won't help you. It will have the opposite effect and, again, could trigger negative thoughts and feelings.
- Speak to your doctor about taking probiotics to help your digestive system get back on track. One of the reasons why your stomach is bloating is due to an imbalance of healthy gut bacteria.
- Time to slow your eating down; if you're a fast eater, you tend to take in air as you eat, which could sit in the stomach and contribute to the bloating.
- What about those scales? Well, it's time to toss those scales into the bin. They have you focus on the one thing you want to avoid: your weight!

POSITIVE CHANGES YOU CAN LOOK FORWARD TO IN YOUR RECOVERY

 Oh, yes, and there are many...

Once you start to follow your structured eating program, there will follow some functional positive, exciting new changes that will happen. These include:

- Beginning to feel calmer as your emotions and mood begin to stabilize.
- Your sleeping will improve; you won't be waking up in the night hungry.
- Feeling so much less anxious and stressed.
- Your skin will become so much brighter due to hormonal and dietary changes.

- Your self-esteem will improve as you start to feel more confident in yourself.

You will see so many exciting new positive changes as you move forward; it will be like you've awakened from a dream or, rather, a nightmare!

YOUR BODY'S NATURAL SETPOINT

Start now and keep moving forward!

Depending on what your weight is when you start your recovery from bulimia, my clients usually end up returning to the same weight as when they began their recovery. So why wait? Why not start now?

For all my clients and me, the fear of putting on weight is the number one main concern; I certainly didn't want to.

I had a warped sense of how I looked and an intense fear that I would be fat after recovery. This overwhelmed me. I would have nightmares.

But the truth is that yes, in the beginning, you may put on some weight temporarily, but once your body adjusts to having food and water regularly and finds its own natural set point again, your weight will settle back down to where you were or close to that before you started your recovery. If you also have anorexia, obviously, an increase in weight is incredibly significant.

What's the body's natural set point?

Your body is predisposed to maintain a certain weight range, which is called your set point. Genetics has a lot to do with what specifically your body's natural set point is, as it depends on:

- Your build
- How tall you are
- Your gender
- Your bone structure
- Your metabolism, etc

 Your body will do what it can to stay within this specific weight range and has unique mechanisms to keep your weight within your natural set point.

It's like your body's own thermostat that regulates your weight level.

When you go below your body's own set point and starve yourself, lots of things happen:

- Your metabolism slows down, and your body goes into the fat storage mode holding on to any fats you may have eaten, storing them in case there's a famine, and no food will be coming, and it will try to use the few calories coming in more effectively.
- Your body then starts to do whatever it can to save your energy.
- You start to feel very tired, wanting to sleep more.
- Both your appetite and metabolism adjust to try to return to your set point.
- Your menstrual cycle may begin to slow down or even stop.

- You may feel cold because your body temperature will drop.
- Your urges to binge and purge could increase as it's your body's way of calling for more food to work properly.

When you go above your body's own set point, and weight is put on. It realizes that it has plenty of food coming in, your body will do the opposite:

- It will try to fight against weight gain by speeding up your metabolism so that energy can be used much faster and more efficiently.
- It knows the energy will be replaced, so it doesn't need to store extra fat reserves.
- It also raises your temperature to try and burn off the extra calories.

For example, holiday weight gain is typical, then once returning home and back to a regular pattern of eating and exercise, the weight will naturally drop back down without much effort to their usual body's natural setpoint.

How do I know where my body's natural set point is?

No test can be taken to find out what your body's natural set point is. But listen clearly to your body's needs and:

- Let go of any thoughts of dieting and restricting your food completely.
- Tune into your hunger and learn only to eat when you're hungry.
- Eat slowly, focusing on all the fabulous flavors and tastes.

- Tune in to the feelings of satisfaction, knowing you now have had enough.

Your body will welcome this pattern and naturally do what's right for you.

How smart is your body! It's a real work of art, like a fine Picasso or Rembrandt.

What you have learned here is that you may put on some weight in your recovery, but this will only be temporary. It's like having money in your purse; it's only temporary!

> **"CHANGE MAY BE HARD IN THE BEGINNING,**
> **MESSY IN THE MIDDLE, AND AMAZING IN**
> **THE END" —ROBIN S. SHARMA**

WATER, WATER, WATER

Why is it important to drink water?

- Your body is made up of approximately 75% water
- The brain is made up of approximately 85% water
- Your blood is made up of approximately 80% water
- Your muscles are made up of approximately 70% water

When we look at these percentages, it's quite incredible how vital water is for our body to function correctly.

What happens when we drink water?

- As the water flows through your body, it delivers nutrients to the cells and carries away waste.

- Water assists the kidneys in flushing the toxins out of the body. When the kidneys are working correctly, other organs like the liver are more in balance.
- Water acts as a cooling system; it moves heat to the body's surface, which is when you sweat.
- Water lubricates your joints, which makes the muscles work more smoothly.

IT'S TIME TO REHYDRATE YOURSELF

 Due to your bingeing and purging, taking laxatives or diuretics, or over-exercising, your body is very dehydrated, which affects every organ of your body.

Research has revealed dehydration is the cause of stress, chronic pain, and many degenerative diseases. It also affects your electrolyte levels, which can cause many side effects. More information on electrolytes is presented later in this step.

THE INTRIGUING DR. BATMAN

Dr. F. Batmmanghelidj, yes, also known as Dr. Batman, the author of *Your Body's Many Cries for Water*, spent most of his life studying the effects water has on the body.

Here are a few intriguing facts from Dr. Batman:

- So many aches and pains that people have every day, including hunger, are actually caused by dehydration.
- If you're thirsty, you're way past thirst, and your body is desperate for water.

- It's virtually impossible to tell the difference between "thirst signal" and authentic hunger.
- If bulimics begin to rehydrate their bodies well and drink water before their food, this problem will disappear. It's time to step up the amount you're drinking! But do so gradually.

How much water should we be drinking per day?

This depends on the individual and their circumstances, including climate and how much they move their body.

The recommended daily intake is:

3.7 liters for men
2.7 liters for women

Signs you are dehydrated:

- If your urine is darker in color, this may be an indication that your kidneys are working harder than they should
- Itchy dry skin and mouth
- Sunken eyes
- Inability to produce tears
- Dizziness
- Weakness and fatigue

Maybe for many years, your body had been chronically dehydrated. This cannot be reversed in a couple of days by drinking a few glasses of water each day. Slowly increase your water intake, regularly drinking throughout the day, building gradually.

ELECTROLYTES

WE SOMETIMES HEAR THE WORD "ELECTROLYTES," BUT WHAT ON EARTH ARE THEY?

Electrolytes are salts in your body, such as potassium, calcium, chloride, and sodium. They're used by your body to:

- Control the correct amount of fluid in your organs and blood vessels.
- Regulate hydration and pH levels as well as nerve and muscle function.

If you're bingeing and purging or taking laxatives, you'll become dehydrated, which then causes electrolyte imbalances.

If we have an imbalance of electrolytes in the body, it can cause:

- Nausea
- Low mood, tiredness
- Low blood pressure
- Muscle spasms and weakness
- An irregular heartbeat
- Trembling
- Aching joints
- In extreme cases, even death. Prolonged and severe electrolyte imbalance can lead to shock, cerebral edema (swelling in the brain), seizures, and coma (*Eating Disorders Review*, 1999).

The most frequent electrolyte imbalances seen in bulimics are:

Reduced sodium levels in the body that can disrupt brain function, causing you to feel:

Nauseous
Irritable
Headachy and fatigued

This information is confirming further the importance of introducing water every day gradually.

LET'S TALK ABOUT SEROTONIN

So, what is serotonin?

Serotonin is a crucial hormone that helps us to balance our feelings, mood, and calmness. It's also known as the happy hormone. Research shows that people with bulimia have low levels of serotonin.

It has many functions:

- It helps parts of the brain to communicate with other parts of the brain and body healthily
- It helps you to sleep
- It works with your digestion
- It helps to control the muscles and how you move
- It influences your bowel movements and appetite

But low levels of serotonin cause feelings of depression, anxiety, cravings for sweet foods, and disrupts your sleep patterns.

To naturally increase your serotonin:

- Spend more time in the sunlight, which could be tricky if you live in the UK in the winter; you're more likely to drown in the rain rather than get sunstroke!
- Exercise helps to boost your serotonin. But exercise within reason.
- Massage helps increase serotonin and dopamine, another mood-related neurotransmitter. It also decreases cortisol, which is a hormone your body produces when you're anxious or stressed.

We want more serotonin!

When your serotonin levels are at a healthy level, you'll feel more emotionally stable, more focused, calmer, and guess what? HAPPIER.

MENSTRUATION

Women, have you noticed changes in your menstruation?

Amenorrhea is the absence of menstruation or monthly periods altogether.

Bulimia may cause your periods to change, to reduce, or even stop. It affects between 7-40% of people with bulimia. If very young, it could delay the start of the first period.

The causes of amenorrhea:

- Extremely low body weight. Depriving your body of the foods it needs to create energy disrupts the hormone cycle that regulates your periods.
- Excessive exercise. Many factors contribute to loss of periods, including low body fat or compulsive exercise.
- Stress. Mental stress can affect your brain that controls your hormones that regulate your periods.

Symptoms of amenorrhea:

- Night sweats
- Sleeping difficulties
- Irritability

If this happens to you, it's essential to seek help from your doctor to determine if any underlying medical conditions exist. But the good news is that for most women, within a few months of recovering from bulimia, their body will correct itself, and ovulation will begin again.

WHAT ABOUT YOUR ZZZZZZ?

Do you get enough sleep? If you're tired, controlling your bingeing and purging can become more difficult. So, it's crucial to look at the amount of sleep you're getting.

Experiment and see how you respond to different amounts of sleep.

According to SleepFoundation.org, teenagers' (14-17) sleep range is 8-10 hours while adults' (18-64) sleep range is 7-9 hours.

If you're struggling to get the correct amount of sleep, follow these simple yet practical, healthy tips to help you sleep all night soundly.

- Get into the routine to keep your bedroom only for sleeping or sex, not to lounge around watching TV, working on your computer, or tinkering on your phone.
- Make a sleep schedule and stick to it even on weekends.
- Avoid daytime naps, as this will affect your night-time sleep pattern.
- Exercise, within reason, daily.
- Beware of too much caffeine or alcohol.
- Build into your bedtime ritual relaxation, like taking a warm bath with candles.

Techniques in this book to help you sleep more soundly right through the night are:

- Emotional Freedom Technique (EFT), also known as the tapping technique, which you'll be learning in Step 8.
- Mindfulness—learning mindfulness would be a massive help to still your never-ending chatter, keeping you awake at night. Imagine a muzzle to silence your leprechaun?
- Thought stopping technique to batter that chatter! In Step 5.

Hypnotherapy is also an incredible therapy to reprogram your unconscious mind to sleep soundly right through the night.

 What we can learn here is that as you gradually introduce your structured meal program over time, your sleep will improve.

"OUR MINDS DISTORT OUR MIRRORS"

"SPIN AND WIN" TECHNIQUE

I want to teach you a fantastic technique to help you to reduce any negative feelings. For this exercise and learning, you're going to focus on the feelings of being scared, such as, that you're going to put on weight or that you can't ever change and be free from bulimia. Whatever the scared feeling is for you right now, we're going to work with it to change the way you feel.

Let's begin:

1.   Think of a situation that triggers the scared feeling. Where does that scared feeling start? Where in your body would be the first time that you're aware of that scared feeling? Quite often, people say in their stomachs, but usually, that's where it ends up, so I really want you to tune in and ask yourself where this scared feeling starts?

Is it in your forehead? Or your throat or in your chest, and then moves to the knot in your stomach? This would be the path of the feeling.

2.   For that scared feeling to remain there, it would have to spin forward or backward or to the right or the left because, geometrically, those are the only two possibilities.

If you aren't sure or if you think it isn't moving at all, then I really want you to tune into that scared feeling and ask yourself which way it's spiraling.

3.   Now take either index finger and move it in a circle clockwise or anticlockwise, whichever way the scared feeling is moving, really get in tune with it. Imagine a circle with arrows, give the circle color, make it red, and spin the circle moving whichever way the scared feeling is moving.

4. Now, reverse the direction of the spin: Now make the circle purple and spin it in the opposite direction, next spin it faster, now faster still, and notice what happens, the scared feeling will start to spin backward faster and lessen.

 Excellent, look at you reprogramming your unconscious mind, and this is a fantastic way to reduce not only the scared feelings but also any negative feelings like anxiety, guilt, fears, or any other strong feeling. (Bandler, 2010).

Video Demonstration Link: https://bulimiasucks.com/spin-win/

EVEN PRINCESS'S DEVELOP BULIMIA!

Prince William said of his mother, Princess Diana, and her struggles with bulimia—admitting he was "proud" of his mum for bringing issues like hers to public attention. He continued, "These things are illnesses, and they need to be treated. Mental health needs to be taken as seriously as physical health."

But Diana herself, in what was pretty forward-thinking for the '80s and '90s, had always spoken frankly about her struggle with food (Mason, 2017).

STEP 6 - HERE ARE YOUR KEY EMPOWERING ACTION STEPS:

- In your recovery, your key golden nugget is to fully understand that if you were to put on weight, it's **NOT** real weight gain. It's not you piling on the pounds. It's the bulimia bloat and **only temporary**. Weight gain is a common symptom of recovery as your body begins to adjust and balance itself out. The good news is that this won't last long; it typically occurs within the first few days and lasts for only a few weeks. But it's important to remember this is your body's way of healing, and it will stop swelling as your body adjusts to your new eating patterns.

- Having learned about the body's natural set point and how it's predisposed to maintain a specific weight range, your body will do what it can to stay within this specific weight range. Your body has unique mechanisms to keep your weight within your natural set point.

- It's time to nourish your body with water due to your bingeing and purging. Your body is desperately dehydrated, which affects every organ, particularly your energy levels and brain function. So it's essential to begin introducing water into your daily life, gradually.

- Now you also have the unique "Spin and Win" technique to help you reduce all your negative feelings about weight increase. Plus, any other feelings that may arise as you continue on your motivational path to freedom, spinning everything and anyone who may get in your way.

- Serotonin, you want more of, so think about how you can naturally begin to raise your serotonin levels.

Having the tools and techniques to set you free is an empowering thought that will inspire and motivate you to stay focused and move on to the next step.

STEP 7

HOW CAN I CHANGE ALL MY NEGATIVE HABITS?

"The secret of success is learning how to use pain and pleasure instead of having pain and pleasure use you. If you do that, you're in control of your life. If you don't, life controls you" —Tony Robbins.

Your empowering learnings from Step 6:

- The "Spin and Win" technique, how powerful is that? It's incredibly effective in reducing not only the scared feelings connected to putting on weight but also any other painful feelings you may be having... So, keep spinning.
- Also, if you were to put on weight in your recovery, it's common. It does happen to the vast majority of people beginning their recovery. But YES, it's only temporary while your body adjusts to your new eating habits and patterns.
- Your body's natural set point regulates your weight level. Your body will do what it can to stay within this specific weight range and has unique mechanisms to do so. Thus, if you were to put weight on in your recovery process, your

body would eventually drop back down to your natural set point. Yeaha! We like that.

- Your water intake should be increasing now, giving you the nourishment your body has been yearning. With that comes so many benefits with copious amounts of new energy, which is an exciting energizing thought in itself.

The positive guidance you'll be learning here in Step 7:

- How you're going to start addressing your habits and patterns as you become even more aware of your evil leprechaun and how he drives your habits.
- Understand the enormous dangers of taking laxatives or diuretics and how you're going to begin to change this behavior for good.
- Compulsive exercising, if you're over-exercising, learn how you can begin to look at, address, and change the drive for this behavior.
- Oh yes, and learn how you can break your habits instantly with the fantastic "Shatter That Habit" technique.

Let's get motivated to move on to Step 7. While using your motivational anchor, pressing your finger and thumb together and briefly imagine how you're going to be in the future free from bulimia forever. Feel that inspiration and motivating force. Allow it to wash over your whole body now. Excellent!

WHAT IS A HABIT?

Habits are sequences of actions that we carry out routinely on autopilot to make our lives easier, acting as shortcuts that allow us to use our energy on more critical areas of our lives. Of course, over time, we've created good positive habits. But, alas, we've also created the not so good habits.

Having bulimia isn't your fault! It's the natural result of your mental programming at this moment in time.

Let me clarify to you that you aren't crazy, as I once thought I was. You've developed some very unsuccessful habits that are contributing to your bulimia pattern. The interesting point here is that once you've changed the way you think and feel with the different techniques, you'll learn to develop new positive habits to guide you successfully toward your freedom.

**LET'S LOOK AT YOUR HABITS AND PULL THAT
RABBIT RIGHT OUT OF YOUR HABIT!**

WHAT HAPPENS TO YOUR BRAIN WHEN YOU BEGIN TO CREATE A NEW HABIT?

Creating a new positive habit can be so powerful and lead you to beneficial and encouraging life changes. We're all creatures of habit. We're relying on our past learned behaviors and habits to make our decisions.

As you create a habit, your brain has developed neuro-pathways that unfold as your automatic, go-to habits.

Here's the exciting part; It's all down to neuroplasticity, meaning your brain's ability to change. Consequently, we can adapt and reorganize how our brains are wired.

Therefore, when creating a new powerful habit, you're also creating new positive neural pathways in your brain. Thus, that old habit = the old neural pathway in your brain becomes weaker. It wears off in time, making room for new neuro pathways to form. That's why it's easier to create a healthy new positive habit than continue the old one.

"NEURONS THAT FIRE TOGETHER, WIRE TOGETHER." CONSEQUENTLY, "NERVES THAT FIRE APART, WIRE APART"

How you created your habits

It takes conscious action and practice to form your habit. Therefore, it takes intentional action and training to break your habit. Or better still, replace it with an excellent positive habit.

Let's begin to understand your habit cycle. You can't change a habit without understanding how they work individually for you. What precisely are the steps?

There are three steps to the process:

- A trigger
- A routine
- A reward

Earlier in the book, you began to identify the specific triggers and rewards of your bulimia. For example, the reasons why you make yourself sick.

Hop back to Step 1, and read through the identified function, rewards, or needs of your behavior. For example, "It's my way to distract me from the stress of daily life."

So, you engage in your habit of bingeing and purging to gain some sort of reward like numbing your emotions, relieving boredom, or time for you.

Examples of rewards:

- Weight loss
- Release of dopamine
- Relief from overeating
- Comfort
- Detachment from feelings

If there's repetition, the habit develops.

LET'S UNDERSTAND WHAT AND HOW DOPAMINE IS LINKED TO YOUR HABITS

Dopamine is a chemical made in the brain and is released when your brain is expecting a reward. It's the "feel good" hormone. So, when you come to associate a particular activity like bingeing and purging with pleasure and reward, this then motivates you to repeat the behavior. Just the mere thought of it could be enough to raise your dopamine levels.

Habit Diary

By identifying your habit behavior that sweeps you into your urges, you can start to break the pattern of this habit. Maintaining them is exceptionally achievable. A great way to do this is to keep a diary of what pattern is connected to your habit.

 Complete the HABIT DIARY table in Step 7, in your workbook. Otherwise, grab your notebook and make your own habit diary based on this example:

Remember, this isn't about changing the habit at this point but becoming aware of the links and triggers that cause the pattern.

For example:

- **Your habit:** Jumping onto the scales first thing in the morning.
- **Where you are:** At home.
- **What you were doing just before the habit:** Getting dressed, jeans feel tighter.
- **Thoughts and feelings/images just before the habit:** *I'm fatter!* Image of bulges over the tops of jeans. Feel angry.
- **Thoughts and feelings/images during the habit:** Panic, scared, worthless.
- **Thoughts and feelings/images after the habit:** *I must not eat anything today!* Feel sad, lonely, and a failure.
- **Your reward/pleasure:** Bingeing and purging.

In this example, let me explain further about the reward, or we could call it the pleasure. Your whole day would be ruined, and the leprechaun would have been nonstop about how worthless, hopeless, and what a failure you are, and oh yes, to gain some relief or pleasure would be to binge and purge.

When completing your habit diary, write everything down when you're aware of the habit rather than at the end of the day, as you can forget what you were thinking and feeling at the time the habit occurred.

NOW THE FUN PART ... TIME TO CREATE A NEW HABIT

Now, you're becoming consciously aware of your habits and rewards. It's time to replace old habits with new ones, and repetition is the key.

The more you repeat your new habit. The more the brain will cement the new neural pathways. Therefore, the more you'll stop the old habit.

Now, start by deciding on one positive habit you would like to create.

Once you've identified your old habit, it's time to decide on the new positive habit you're going to create.

Starting with a small habit will allow you to be better prepared, see your focus more clearly, feel more motivated, and it will be more manageable and achievable.

The key is to be specific and break down the big picture of your new habit you're going to create. Here's an example of breaking that habit goal down, so it's more achievable:

"I want to stop stressing about everything."
"I want to stop weighing myself."

These probably aren't going to become real habits, as they are too vague. It's time to break that picture down into smaller chunks. For example:

"When I get home from work, the first thing I'm going to do is change into my walking clothes/shoes and take a 30-minute walk to relieve my stresses of the day."

Or "I am only going to weigh myself once a day or every other day."

These are better because they're more accurate.

It's time to commit to making the change

It may have taken you some time to create the old habit, so this isn't an overnight fix. It will take some time. So, make that commitment, because if you aren't going to do it, then no one else can! You can do this. But you have to decide you're going to give this your full attention and commit to making this change.

Okay, so now you've identified your habits and rewards, excellent!

Your steps to changing your habits.

- Repetition is the key to creating this new habit.
- Staying inspired to focus on your new habit may not be so easy at the start. But it's essential to take one day at a time.
- Imagine how you might be in two months from now, having achieved your goal of changing this habit?
- Tell friends and family of your intentions to help reinforce and encourage you to stay focused.

Remember, your brain can change; there are no limits to what it can do and how it can help you to free you from bulimia.

How long does it take to create a new habit?

In the past, psychologists believed it took 21 days to create a new habit. New research shows that it takes 66 days to develop useful new positive habits. Of course, everyone is wired differently; for you, it could be less.

Here's how to break your unwanted habit with:

"SHATTER THAT HABIT" TECHNIQUE

This is a new technique to help you to stay motivated and change your habit permanently.

You'll be stepping out of the old you and then seeing yourself how you would like to be in the future, making that image so powerful that it attracts you to become drawn into the kind of person who is free from that old harmful habit.

Here we go with the powerful habit changer:

1. Now that you've identified your habit, I want you to visualize yourself doing that habit, including what happens just before this habit begins. Step into this image, looking through your own eyes. Set that picture aside. This is your trigger picture.
2. Now create your new positive habit. Make an image of this. Make it large, bright, and colorful of yourself already having this new habit. In this image, you can really see you spar-

kle. Your posture has changed, and you look happy and relaxed. What would you be saying to yourself? How would you look? Feel? Now, reduce that image, shrinking it to a small dot.

3. Now bring forward the old and the new habit. Then when you're ready, imagine yourself participating in the old habit.

4. Now, have the new habit picture rapidly explode and fly into the image of you doing the harmful habit. See that old habit smash into minuscule pieces as you say the word "swishhhhh" with the new positive habit image replacing the old habit image.

5. Now blank the screen as if the TV has lost its connection.

6. Repeat the process faster this time. As you do this, the new positive habit image comes alive with you happy, positively practicing your new habit as the negative image loses color and fades away into the far distance.

7. Swish Swish Swish. Keep repeating the whole process at least five more times, getting faster each time.

Then repeat the whole process twice a day, morning and night, until the good habit becomes embedded and you're no longer unconsciously doing the bad habit.

 Fantastic, stay focused, and enjoy the challenge of changing your habits.

Video Demonstration Link: https://bulimiasucks.com/shatter-that-habit/

Talking of habits, do you have a habit of taking laxatives?

LAXATIVES

What are they?

A laxative is a medication taken for constipation, working with the large intestine to trigger a bowel movement. My clients with bulimia think this is going to help them become thinner. But, alas, this isn't the case.

You may think that abusing the body and taking laxatives is going to get rid of the food and calories you've binged on before the body can absorb any calories. Laxatives drain your body of water, electrolytes, and minerals like potassium, sodium, and magnesium.

But it's essential to understand that laxatives work on your large intestines. Most of the foods and calories eaten are absorbed into the body in the small intestines before it reaches the large intestines. Therefore, it's not going to help you become thinner.

Taking laxatives to become thinner is so much more harmful to the body instead of making you slimmer. I know once you've taken the laxatives, your stomach may be flatter, you feel lighter, and those scales may make you happier. But it's only temporary, as you've only lost fluid from the body.

Once you drink fluids and rehydrate your body, what happens? Yes, you'll be back to where you started.

And because the body builds a tolerance to the laxatives, for many, the cycle continues, increasing the laxatives, the pattern worsens, and they become severely dehydrated.

What are the dangers of taking laxatives?

1. Dehydration is one of the leading causes of laxative abuse. Taking laxatives causes diarrhea, which is mostly water in your bowel movements. To compensate, you may just drink more water. But, unfortunately, this doesn't work, as the body doesn't hydrate fast enough. Therefore, it can cause dizziness, feeling faint, confused, weakness, blurred vision, and can lead to organ failure and death.

2. Electrolyte Imbalance. Dehydration affects the loss of electrolyte minerals in the body, for example, potassium, sodium, calcium, magnesium, and phosphorus. These electrolytes help to maintain your muscles, nerve, and heart functions.

3. Depression. If you have bulimia and are abusing laxatives, then you could be feeling very low, even depressed. Abusing laxatives will increase the feelings of depression and tiredness due to the low levels of electrolytes in the body.

4. Constipation. So how does this work? You're taking the laxatives to get the bowels moving, so how does it cause constipation? This is a good question. The answer is the overuse of laxatives damages your colon by artificially stimulating it, and your nerves become weakened and damaged, thus causing the constipation.

5. Bleeding in the stools. Because of the misuse of laxatives and diarrhea and always having to rush to the bathroom, the anus and rectum can become aggravated and cause bowel movements to become sore, painful, and bleed. You may become aware of blood in your stools due to extreme overuse of laxatives, which could result in anemia. Anemia symptoms can include dizziness, absolute exhaustion, irregular heartbeat, and chest pain.

6.   Increased risk of colon cancer. Excessive use of laxatives can severely damage the nerve lining of your colon, which could become weak and not work correctly. It may also cause IBS and, if this continues, colon failure, which may result in surgical removal of part or the whole of your colon, resulting in a colostomy. Therefore, it could also increase your risk of getting colon cancer due to the constant irritation, swelling, and inflammation caused by the laxatives, affecting the cells, which could develop abnormalities.

7.   Bingeing and purging increases if you're also using laxatives. Many of the side effects like feeling fat, bloated, tired, or down, are triggers that cause you to binge. So, it sends you into the downward spiral of the binge-purge cycle.

8.   Kidney Damage. Your kidneys work so hard to remove waste from your body and filter your blood. To work correctly, they need plenty of fluids. As you become dehydrated, the toxins won't be flushed from the body, which could lead to serious kidney damage. If severe, it could lead to kidney failure.

LAXATIVES AND THE BULIMIA BEAST

Bloating, oh yes, the dreaded bloating can be caused by the use of laxatives because:

- Again, due to dehydrated, the body slips into the panic mode, slowing digestion and holding onto any fluids, causing bloating.
- Laxatives trap gases in the intestines, which can also cause you to feel bloated.

NOW IS THE TIME TO STOP ABUSING LAXATIVES

Are you in the vicious circle of taking laxatives to feel slimmer or lose weight only to fall back down into that rabbit hole of feeling fat and bloated because of extreme water retention then trying to climb out of that rabbit hole by taking more laxatives?

Well, now is the time to begin to make that change and stop abusing your body with laxatives; the physical and mental effects are extremely dangerous.

Please consult your doctor about safe methods of quitting laxative abuse.

It all comes back to your thoughts and feelings that drive this behavior.

 Complete the LAXATIVE CAUSES & NEW COPING STRATEGIES table in Step 7, in your workbook. Otherwise, grab your notebook and complete this list of your thoughts and feelings that cause your behavior of taking laxatives. Now is the time to challenge these. Once you have your list, then create new powerful positive coping strategies.

LAXATIVE CAUSES & NEW COPING STRATEGIES:

THE CAUSES   NEW COPING STRATEGIES

 Great, so now you have your list of what causes you to reach for the laxatives and listed new coping strategies, it's time to STOP, STOP, STOP taking laxatives. There are so many dangerous health effects which, if they become extreme, could lead to death. TOSS THOSE PILLS IN THE BIN NOW! Yes, this may be a scary thought. But you can do this and move on completely.

Here are positive steps to begin to break your vicious laxative circle.

1. It's time to start to hydrate your body, so begin drinking half a liter, to begin with gradually building up to 2 plus liters of water per day, little and often is best, and avoid beverages with caffeine, as this is a diuretic. It's essential to not only drink at regular intervals but also to eat regularly, of course! So, hop back to Step 4, learn about how to implement your structured eating program.

2. Start to move your body more. Do some physical activity each day. Take a 20-minute walk. It will help to stimulate your digestion and get your bowels moving again. I am

not asking you to take this to the extreme and rush out and spend the day like a rabbit, hopping in and out of every aerobic exercise class you can find at your gym. This will exacerbate specific side effects like constipation. Start with gentle walking.

3. As I mentioned, there could be side effects when stopping laxatives. Or there might not be any! Constipation, pain, and bloating, to mention a few, are possibilities, but this doesn't mean you'll get any. If you do, it's important to remember that they're only temporary and will stop.

4. Inform a friend or family member you have made this decision to completely stop taking laxatives. Having the support and someone to be accountable to will increase your chances of achieving your goal of breaking free from laxative abuse.

5. It's now time to step up the fiber. To get your bowels moving naturally, you need to eat fiber. It moves quickly and relatively easily through your digestive tract and helps it to function correctly.

Men should aim for 30 to 38 grams of fiber a day.
Women should aim for 21 to 25 grams of fiber a day.
These sorts of foods include whole-grain bread, cereals, and crackers—grains with wheat bran.

High fiber fruits:

Pear	5.5 grams (1 medium)
Bananas	3.0 grams (1 medium)
Apples with skin	4.5 grams (1 medium)
Oranges without skin!	3.0 grams (1 medium)
Strawberries	3.0 grams (1 cup)
Raspberries	8.0 grams (1 cup)

High fiber vegetables:

Green peas boiled	9.0 grams (1 cup)
Broccoli boiled	5.0 grams (1 cup)
A potato baked with skin	4.0 grams (1 medium)
Sweet corn boiled	3.5 grams (1 cup)
Cauliflower raw	2.0 grams (1 cup)
Carrot raw	1.5 grams (1 medium)

The darker the greens, the higher the fiber content.

Avoid prunes, as they're an irritant laxative. If you were to dive in and eat lots of prunes, it could have the same negative results as if you were taking laxatives.

6. Speak to a nutritionist. They will be able to help you to figure out good positive eating habits, which will help to prevent bingeing.

7. When you begin to break free from the laxatives, write down the frequency of your bowel movements. If you find you're constipated for more than three days, it's time to call your doctor.

So, toss those laxatives in the bin along with your scales and start now to increase your water intake. Begin on your structured eating program. Trust me; your body will rejoice with all the fabulous nutrients.

The techniques you have learned so far in this book can help you to begin to address your laxative abuse. For example:

"The New You" technique from Step 1.

"Electrify your motivation" technique from Step 2.

"Instant trigger change" technique from Step 2.

"Shrink and blink" technique also from Step 2.

"New belief" technique from Step 5.

"Thought stopping" technique also from Step 5.

The "Spin and Win" technique from Step 6.

 Think about this list and identify which techniques are going to help you break through your laxative abuse and address this pattern healthily.

DIURETIC ABUSE

Diuretics are also known as "water pills." So, with a name like that, that's exactly what they do! They rid your body of fluids, increasing the frequency of how often you need to pass urine and removing all that energizing water and salts from your body.

In eating disorders, diuretic abuse is a form of purging. Like laxative abuse, my clients believe that taking "water tablets" will rid their body of the foods and calories after a binge, making them feel thinner until they start to rehydrate their body. Then they're back to where they started.

If you're taking diuretics, the body can start to hold on to water, which, in turn, will cause you to gain water weight.

Some side effects of diuretic abuse include:

- Muscle cramps/weakness

- Fainting, dizziness, headaches, and confusion
- Nausea
- Risk of seizures
- Irregular heartbeat
- Very low blood pressure
- Extreme thirst
- Constipation
- Joint disorders (gout)
- Impotence
- Kidney damage
- Electrolyte imbalances
- Edema (swelling in certain parts of the body)

It all comes back to your thoughts and feelings that drive this behavior.

Complete the DIURETICS CAUSES & NEW COPING STRATEGIES table in Step 7, in your workbook. Otherwise, grab your notebook and complete this list of your thoughts and feelings that cause your behavior of taking diuretics. Now is the time to challenge these. Once you have your list, then create new powerful positive coping strategies.

DIURETICS CAUSES & NEW COPING STRATEGIES:

THE CAUSES   **NEW COPING STRATEGIES**

Now is the time to stop, stop, stop taking these water tablets; they're severely harming your body.

The techniques you have learned so far in this book can help you begin to address your diuretic abuse. For example:

"The New You" technique from Step 1.

"Electrify your motivation" technique from Step 2.

"Instant trigger change" technique from Step 2.

"Shrink and blink" technique also from Step 2.

"New belief" technique from Step 5.

"Thought stopping" technique also from Step 5.

The "Spin and Win" technique from Step 6.

So go back to these techniques and see which ones are going to help you begin to break this habit, maybe only two or maybe all of them?

COMPULSIVE EXERCISING

In the media and society itself, people are always trumpeting the health benefits of regular exercise, so this can be difficult to avoid if you're struggling with compulsive exercise.

Some of my clients feel they can only eat if they're overexercising, and if this isn't possible, immense feelings of guilt, anxiety, irritability, and distress overwhelm them.

Many people go crazy with exercise to try and control their weight. At every given opportunity, they're exercising like a never-ending hamster on a wheel. But your body needs time to heal between exercise sessions.

Are you over-exercising? Let's look at warning signs to identify if your relationship with exercise is unhealthy:

No flexibility in your exercise routine?

Does the guilt, anxiety, distress flood in if your routine is delayed or interrupted?

If you're ill or have an injury, is the need to exercise greater than rest?

Never having a rest day?

Due to exercise avoiding school, work, or social events?

If you can relate to any of the above, then it's time to start to address your behaviors.

What problems can compulsive exercise cause?

Let me explain, so you have a clear understanding of why you need to change this immense pressure to exercise.

With energy supplies depleted from overexercise and/or lack of food:

- Your bones become weak, which could cause bone fractures.
- It could affect your heart and lead to heart failure.
- For girls and women, a loss of menstrual period.
- You experience unhealthy weight loss.
- Here comes the dehydration again! Your body will become too dehydrated, and that can cause many issues from blurred vision, dizziness, confusion, feeling faint, which could lead to organ failure and even death.

 Compulsive exercising can increase your anxiety and stress levels with the pressure you put on yourself. So, to begin to break free from compulsive exercise, start to identify the specific parts of your relationship to exercise that are problematic for you.

ITS TIME BECOME AWARE OF YOUR BEHAVIOUR

Looking at what's causing you to overexercise:

What thoughts are driving you to overexercise? Oh yes, there could be a multitude of these beasts.

For example:

"I had that donut at break time, so I must work out for longer."

"I'm looking fat today, so I must work out harder."

"I feel worthless, and exercise makes me feel more confident."

"It helps to reduce my anxiety and calms me."

"When I exercise, if I don't feel completely exhausted at the end, then I'm not perfect."

Therefore, this extreme pressure to increase the length or difficulty of their exercise routine intensifies.

Oh yes, these darn thoughts... It's back to that leprechaun and his devious whisperings that need to be addressed. So, tune into what thoughts and feelings you're trying to mask by overexercising?

It all comes back to your thoughts and feelings that drive this behavior.

Complete the OVER - EXERCISE CAUSES & NEW COPING STRATEGIES table in Step 7, in your workbook. Otherwise, grab your notebook and complete this list of your thoughts and feelings that cause your behavior of over-exercising. Now is the time to challenge these. Once you have your list, then create new powerful positive coping strategies.

OVER - EXERCISE CAUSES & NEW COPING STRATEGIES:

THE CAUSES   **NEW COPING STRATEGIES**

Then once you have your list, it's time to address how you can change this pattern and complete it in the same table. For example:

- Reduce the length of time you exercise by 10 minutes, to begin with.
- Cut back on the number of aerobic classes per week.
- Add one rest day to your week.

Just the thought of reducing the amount of exercise may cause feelings of panic or stress, but this will only be temporary, and as you take this slowly, the more you challenge your patterns, the easier it will become over time.

Rather than exercising, what else could you do? What feelings are you trying to block, replace, squash? Adopt your new coping strategies to replace the old feelings you're striving to achieve by exercising.

 Now is the time to stop, stop, stop over-exercising; it's severely harming your body.

The techniques you have learned so far in this book can help you to begin to address your overexercising. For example:

"The New You" technique from Step 1.

"Electrify your motivation" technique from Step 2.

"Instant trigger change" technique from Step 2.

"Shrink and blink" technique also from Step 2.

"New belief" technique from Step 5.

"Thought stopping" technique also from Step 5.

The "Spin and Win" technique from Step 6.

 Think about this list and identify which techniques are going to help you break through your compulsion to exercise and address this pattern healthily.

"NO MATTER WHAT YOU'RE GOING THROUGH THERE'S A LIGHT AT THE END OF THE TUNNEL" —DEMI LOVATO

SCALES

Talking of habits, do you have a habit of weighing yourself on those dreaded scales more than you should?

Many of my clients weigh themselves every day, sometimes 20 plus times a day. For some, their scales become an obsession and rule their life. I know, as I was like a crazed kangaroo, hopping on and off multiple times a day.

Are they helping you to become thinner? Or do they just ruin your day?

SO, IT IS TIME TO TOSS THOSE SCALES IN THE BIN NOW!

This may sound scary. Yes, I understand this. But there are other ways of telling how you're doing with your weight, such as, ideally, from the way your clothes fit.

Your scales have you focus on the one thing that you don't want to be focusing on, yes, your weight. You don't need a piece of metal to cause you to feel terrible about yourself, to ruin our whole day, and drive you to binge and purge. You do that yourself! Your scales are just another way to drive your mind crazy with uncontrollable thoughts.

Now is the time for you to learn how to hop off your scales into a new constructive direction, leaving your scales to go rusty as you take back control of your life.

o, what do the scales actually weigh?

When you stand on scales, they aren't just weighing fat, but that whole lovely you, your bones, muscles, water, and your weight and can change for so many biological reasons; for example, throughout the month, women retain more water.

> "It's time to change that tale and make a new wish.
> Out with the scales, you are not a fish!"

Toss those scales in the ocean where they belong.

You could either continue to allow that numbered beast to control your life, or you can seriously begin here, today, to learn how to change this behavior once and for all. By reading through all the techniques in this book, you can free yourself of the tight grasp that bulimia has over you.

By making this critical decision to toss those scales into the ocean where they belong, you can then:

1. Relax! Yes, this thought may be initially challenging and scary. But it's one way you can free yourself from the self-punishment you put yourself through every time you step on them.
2. Letting go of this destructive habit of weighing yourself will assist you in releasing some of the thought triggers that are connected to the shame of weight gain that sends you into that downward spiral of bingeing and purging.

Okay, so zip back and batter this habit with the "Shatter That Habit" technique earlier in this step.

Freeing yourself of this habit and the control the scales have is a significant decision that will help propel you into your recovery.

KESHA—AMERICAN SINGER SAYS:

"My whole message is to love who you are and accept all your beautiful imperfections," says the singer. "When I felt I was slipping into unloving territory with myself, I knew I had to listen to my own advice and correct it." Later on, she added, "The decision to take control of it is the scariest thing I've ever done, and this is coming from someone who dives with sharks and jumps out of airplanes for fun." Pretty brave, if we do say so ourselves (Barnes, 2015).

Wow, look how far you've come and the tremendous dynamic learnings about your habits and patterns, empowering you to take back control of your life step by step.

STEP 7 - HERE ARE YOUR KEY EMPOWERING ACTION STEPS:

- Learn your habits, and as you become even more aware of your devious leprechaun's whisperings as he grips your shoulder, driving you to your habit, the more you can shout back at him, beat him off your shoulder, and take back control of your life.
- Laxatives, diuretic abuse, and over-exercise all must be addressed if you're going to continue on your road to recovery. Work through the techniques you've learned so far. Plus, there are more incredible techniques to come as you continue reading through the steps. Reach out for help from a trusted friend or family member.
- Changing your old negative habits with the "Shatter That Habit" technique is unbelievably inspirational. As you become aware of new habits, continue filling out your habit table to learn precisely how your pattern unfolds.
- Time to toss your scales in the ocean. Start to break this pattern with the "Shatter That Habit" technique.

You are amazing and deserve to be free from bulimia. That's why I wrote this book to give you incredibly powerful tools to change all the different areas in your life connected to your bulimia because you can change and become bulimia free.

Remember to increase your self—determination, keep using your "Electrify your Motivation" anchor to help you to stay on this pathway to freedom.

STEP 8

ARE YOU SCARED ABOUT THE CHANGES? THIS STEP IS ALL ABOUT TAPPING!

IT'S TIME TO LEARN A FANTASTIC TECHNIQUE CALLED EFT (EMOTIONAL FREEDOM TECHNIQUE or THE TAPPING TECHNIQUE) TO REDUCE ANY SCARED FEELINGS YOU MAY BE HAVING ABOUT YOUR CHANGES

"IN ANY GIVEN MOMENT, WE HAVE TWO OPTIONS: TO STEP FORWARD INTO GROWTH OR TO STEP BACK INTO SAFETY. IT'S TIME TO TAKE THAT FIRST STEP FORWARD" —ABRAHAM MASLOW

Your empowering learnings from Step 7:

- Taking your powerful learnings so far from Step 7, embrace the change of your new habits as they unfold before you, moment by moment. Listing any new habits, you become aware of as you continue running through the technique "Shatter That Habit." With each change you make, you take back a little more control of your life, finally allowing you to start to control your bulimia rather than it controlling you. Fantastic, look how clever you are.

- Having started to address your laxative, diuretic, and over-exercise abuse, you've begun to change these habits gradually with such an empowering feeling as you propel forward to changing positively.
- Begin to break the habit of scale hopping, slowly reducing the number of times you weigh yourself until you feel confident enough to toss those scales in the ocean.

The positive guidance you'll be learning here in Step 8:

- How would you like to be able to turn toward your fearful, scared, negative feelings, knowing you can instantly reduce them? Yesssss, this is what you're going to learn in this step.
- Where's your motivation to move forward? Oh yes, keep electrifying your motivation to help you through each step.

ARE YOU READY OR NOT READY TO CHANGE?

If you're ready for change, I'm so excited for you. But if you aren't ready for the transition to begin your recovery, if it feels like a mountain of huge emotions around you, making that decision to change have piled up in front of you, I'm here to tell you it's okay. Most of my clients feel or have felt the same. They didn't know how to change or even want to recover.

I get it. At the moment, this is the only way you know how to cope with your life. Your bulimia is serving a purpose for you, even though it's a negative one.

There's part of you that's still getting many different benefits from it.

These benefits could be:

- Maybe you can depend on it. It's that friend or leprechaun sitting there on your shoulder, constantly abusing you, but who would never reject you.
- It's your way to avoid social situations that could provoke anxiety.
- It's your way of punishing yourself because of your negative beliefs.
- It's the one thing you know, and, let's be honest, you're good at it!

There could be a multitude of reasons why you're staying in this binge-purge pattern. But until you make that decision to change, step by step, you'll never break free.

As you discover the different techniques in this book to help you break down your mountain and figure out where to begin to start your new life. You can then start to reprogram your mind to think differently, changing all your negative patterns for positive self-empowering thoughts and feelings. So, keep reading and learning.

"ITS NOW TIME TO DIG OUT YOUR COURAGE AND LEARN TO NOURISH SO YOU CAN TRULY UNFOLD AND FULLY FLOURISH" —KATE HUDSON-HALL

YOUR LEAP TO CHANGE WITH EFT (EMOTIONAL FREEDOM TECHNIQUE)

Before we begin to address your multitude of scared feelings, negative thoughts, and worries you're having right now, I'm going to teach you a specific technique called Emotional Freedom Technique (EFT for short or the tapping technique.)

EFT therapy is a simple yet very powerful way to overcome any painful feelings or emotions that are stopping you from beginning to break free from your old past urges and patterns. It's a fantastic tool to have in your pocket for any negative feelings at any time.

Let me tell you now that it's very bizarre. But it's incredibly powerful in reducing any undesirable feelings you may be having. It's described as acupuncture but without the needles. It involves you tapping on acupressure points on the body while thinking about any negative behavior, feeling, or habit that you want to stop or change.

Also, the great thing about EFT is that you don't have to believe in it! Just follow each step. Learn them and use them, as it works in a powerful way.

It's a very safe and gentle tapping procedure. Using just your fingertips to tap directly on points on your face and body.

How Does EFT Work?

EFT works with your body's energy, which flows through your body along pathways called meridians. Disruptions in our energy creates negative feelings and behavior patterns. Once you find those energy disruptions, you use the tapping process to correct them with focused wording as you tap on nine specific points on the face and body.

Your focused wording helps you to tune in to the painful thought or feeling, which points you to the energy disruptions that you're going to change and reduce. As you tune in to your specific issue, the tapping stimulates the energy pathways and balances your energy disruptions.

What are the benefits of using EFT?

So many of my clients have hugely benefited from tapping whenever they have any negative feelings. They're amazed by how quickly this process can reduce these horrific feelings they may be having.

The good news is by learning EFT:

- It's a quick therapy, and you won't need to relive painful memories.
- Once you've learned the points, you can tap on any difficult feelings.
- You can take it with you wherever you go if you're feeling uneasy. You can just do a round of tapping to reduce the uncomfortable feeling.
- It only takes minutes to dissolve negative feelings.
- The success rate is approximately 90%.
- This is a safe process with no side effects. You can use this process at home, anywhere, any time to bring about immediate relief.

With EFT, you can:

- Dissolve your negative feelings or thoughts, anxieties, and your scared feelings.
- Overcome fears, such as moving forward and begin to make good positive changes to freedom.
- Take back control of the many negative thoughts you may be having about taking that first step and putting weight on. By tapping, you can change the way you feel about those fears.
- Boost your motivation if you're losing motivation to focus on your new positive path.
- Decrease all your specific triggers and urges to binge and purge.
- Resolve cravings to food.
- Build self-confidence.
- Restore inner calm.

So, are you ready to learn this fantastic technique to help you begin changing how you're feeling? It's so exciting. It's such an excellent tool to use anytime you're having any sort of destructive feelings.

HERES HOW YOU ARE GOING TO CHANGE NOW WITH EFT:

Using the fingertips of your index and middle finger of either hand, you tap approximately 5-7 times on each point.

Firmly but gently tap either side of the body as outlined below:

KC: The Karate Chop point (abbreviated KC). This is located at the center of the fleshy part of the outside of your hand (either hand), between the top of the wrist and the base of the baby finger. Or the part of your hand you would use to deliver a karate chop.

EB: At the beginning of the eyebrow just above and to one side of the nose.

SE: On the bone bordering the outside corner of the eye, on the side of the eye.

UE: On the bone under an eye about 1 inch below your pupil. Under the Eye.

UN: On the small area between the bottom of your nose and the top of your upper lip. Under the Nose.

CH: Midway between the point of your chin and the bottom of your lower lip. Even though it's not directly on the point of the chin, we call it the chin point because it's descriptive enough for people to understand easily.

CB: The junction where the sternum (breastbone), collarbone, and the first rib meet. To locate it, first, place your forefinger on the U-shaped notch at the top of the breastbone (about where a man would knot his tie). From the bottom of the U, move your forefinger down toward the navel 1 inch and then go to the left (or right) 1 inch. This point is abbreviated CB for collarbone even though it's not on the collarbone (or clavicle) per se. It's at the beginning of the collarbone, and we call it the collarbone point because that's a lot easier to say than "the junction where the sternum (breastbone), collarbone and the first rib meet."

UA: On the side of the body, at a point even with the nipple (for men) or in the middle of the bra strap (for women). It's about 4 inches below the armpit.

TOH: On the top of the head. If you were to draw a line from one ear, over the head, to the other ear, and another line from your nose to the back of your neck, the TOH point is where those two lines would intersect.

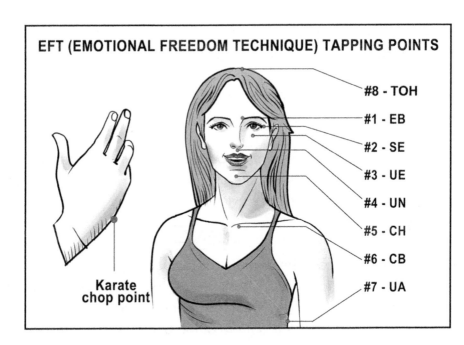

EFT (EMOTIONAL FREEDOM TECHNIQUE) TAPPING POINTS

#8 - TOH
#1 - EB
#2 - SE
#3 - UE
#4 - UN
#5 - CH
#6 - CB
#7 - UA

Karate chop point

The 5 Steps of The EFT Tapping Basic Recipe

1.   Identify the specific feeling that you're going to tap on. (Only focus on one particular negativity at a time). Examples might be, feeling scared, hopeless, worthless, guilty, or shameful, although you could tap on any negative feeling you're having.

2.   Test the initial intensity: I want you to think of a scale between 0–10, with 0 being the feeling has gone entirely and 10 being at its most intense. This gives you a guide, as you'll review your scale after each round of tapping to compare the progress.

If you're tapping on a feeling, you can recreate the memories in your imagination to make it easier to gauge where you would be on the scale.

If you're tapping on physical pain, tune into the pain, and assess the level.

3.   The next step is to repeat a simple phrase while tapping continuously on your karate chop point (KC). You would do this by saying:

"Even though I have this_____, I deeply and completely accept myself."

Fill in the blank for whatever specific emotion you're working on.

For example:

- Even though I feel embarrassed and disgusted with myself, I deeply and completely accept myself.
- Even though these urges are so overwhelming, I deeply and completely accept myself.
- Even though I'm a failure, I deeply and completely accept myself.
- Even though bingeing and purging is my secret, and I'm so disgusted with myself, I deeply and completely accept myself.
- Even though I feel I have no control over my bingeing and purging, I deeply and completely accept myself.

- Even though I'm scared of anyone finding out because they would reject me, I deeply and completely accept myself.

People, People, this is important.

 You may be wondering why we're focusing on the negative here. This is important because the negative creates the energy disruptions that your tapping is going to clear to get that energy flowing naturally again. It allows our calm positivity to bubble up to the surface.

4.   Next, we're going to move on to tapping on each of the points listed above while saying a reminder phrase. So rather than saying the whole long phrase as you've just done tapping on your karate chop point. You're going to reduce it to one or two words. For example, "these urges," "failure," "no control," "I'm scared," anything that's going to help you to stay tuned in to your issue.

Here's the list of the points below:

Beginning of the Eyebrow (EB)
Side of the Eye (SE)
Under the Eye (UE)
Under the Nose (UN)
Chin Point (CH)
Beginning of the Collarbone (CB)
Under the Arm (UA)
Top of the Head (TOH)

5.   Now go back to your scale and see where you are and how the issue has reduced in intensity.

If you aren't down to zero, then repeat the process until you either achieve zero or plateau at some level.

Fantastic, this is so simple to learn, and once you've learned the points and how this process works, it's an incredible way to reduce those negative thoughts and feelings, as you can tap on whatever feelings you have. But be as specific as possible when focusing on your feelings.

I've found EFT to be extremely useful in treating the many issues connected to bulimia and other eating disorders. Anger problems, anxiety disorders, and stress in particular, especially where clients have tried other treatments that haven't been successful (Craig & Craig, n.d.).

Video Demonstration Link: https://bulimiasucks.com/emotional-freedom-technique/

WHEN YOU THINK ABOUT TAKING STEPS TOWARDS CHANGING, WHAT SCARES YOU?

Now that you've learned the process of EFT, you're going to put this into practice. It's an incredible way to reduce your scared thoughts and feelings... so listen up... about living life without bulimia.

So, when you think about changing, what scares you? What's stopping you from moving forward to change?

Complete the SCARED THOUGHTS AND FEELINGS table in Step 8, in your workbook. Otherwise, grab your notebook and make your list.

SCARED THOUGHTS AND FEELINGS	SCALE BEFORE	SCALE AFTER

It's essential to address all the different thoughts and feelings that come with the word "scared."

I'M SCARED OF:

Here's a list of some of the concerns I've worked through with my clients.

1.   I'm scared to live without bulimia.

For you, bulimia may have become your identity. It's part of your life. It drives your actions and behaviors, influencing all your thoughts.

Or it might be as a safety blanket. It's the shield you use to protect yourself. Does it affect how you see yourself and the world around you?

Therefore, the thought of living without it may terrify you. Even though part of you wants to be free from bulimia, another part is scared to live without it. You may have tried in the past with thoughts of stopping, but the fear and panic come rushing back.

I want you to know you aren't alone. This is a familiar feeling of my clients with bulimia.

It may feel overwhelming to discover who you are. But as you become curious, questioning why you do what you do, you can start to break free from your old destructive thinking. Begin now to tune into what you're telling yourself because most of it isn't true.

It's your choice if you listen to your leprechaun's cynical rantings or focus on that new positive you. You get to decide who you are, not your bulimia.

Complete the SCARED OF LIVING WITHOUT table in Step 8, in your workbook. Otherwise, grab your notebook and ask yourself:

What precisely are you scared of living without, yes, your behavior, but what specifically?

Keep going until you have a list of the many reasons why you're scared. Then I want you to begin with your new tapping skill. Start with your scale first and continue rounds of tapping until you're down to a 0.

For example:

"Even though I am scared of all my feelings, I deeply accept myself."

"Even though bingeing and purging are my only way to cope with life, I deeply accept myself."

If you aren't sure what you're scared of living without, that's okay. Tap on:

"Even though I don't know why I'm scared of living without bulimia, I deeply accept myself."

Then ask yourself again the original question, and this time it will be clearer to see what you're scared of, living without bulimia.

"IMAGINE LIVING IN FULL COLOR RATHER THAN THE STALE BLACK AND WHITE"

2.   I'm scared of living with bulimia.

Yes, you absolutely may be scared of continuing to live with all these negative habits, patterns of bingeing and purging, and wishing you were someone else, knowing how it's damaging your body and your whole life.

But this doesn't mean you have to continue this way. It's your choice if you carry on thinking and behaving this way or start to change small patterns of thinking. And if you did, what would you change first?

So, now is the time to begin to believe you're worth fighting for. You deserve a happy life. The journey you'll take to get to that happiness may be easier than you think. Trust that your freedom may be scary because it's new, not because it's bad.

It could be exciting knowing that, by taking that first step, you've moved forward toward your ultimate goal of freedom from bulimia.

 Complete the SCARED OF LIVING WITH BULIMIA table in Step 8, in your workbook. Otherwise, grab your notebook and ask yourself this question:

What specifically are you scared of living with bulimia?

Once again, you have your list; now start tapping, working through your list and reducing what thoughts and feelings come up until you have each one down to a 0.

For example:

"Even though I'm scared of living with bulimia, I deeply accept myself."

"Even though I know I'm damaging my body but can't stop, I deeply accept myself."

Again, if you aren't sure why you're scared of living with bulimia, tap on this.

"Even though I don't know why I'm scared of living with bulimia, I deeply accept myself."

Then ask yourself the original question and tap on what comes up.

"REMEMBER, IF YOU DO WHAT YOU'VE ALWAYS DONE, YOU'LL GET WHAT YOU'VE ALWAYS GOT" —TONY ROBBINS

3. I'm scared of losing control.

There may be many thoughts and feelings that come with losing control when you take that first step to recovery. But you do know how to be in control of you. You have done it before the bulimia and all the negative patterns started. It's there inside you, holding on waiting for you to make that decision.

Recovery is all about change. Sometimes, the change may not be very comfortable. But as you're focusing on how you want to be in the future, the greater the reward will be.

Rather than viewing this as starting over, view it as a blank learning slate to build on beginning to feel better about yourself slowly. Learn to be curious rather than judgmental and critical of yourself. Begin to uncover patterns in your feelings and behaviors so you can learn to change them and be healthier and happier.

 Complete the I'M SCARED OF LOSING CONTROL table in Step 8, in your workbook. Otherwise, grab your notebook and ask yourself this question:

In your notebook, ask yourself this question:

What specifically are you scared of if you lose control?

For example:

"Even though I'm scared I'll lose control without bulimia, I deeply accept myself."

"Even though I might binge and purge if I lose control, I deeply accept myself."

Again, if you aren't sure what you're scared of, if you lose control, tap on this.

"Even though I don't know why I'm scared of losing control, I deeply accept myself."

Then ask yourself the original question and tap on what comes up.

4. I'm scared of who I am without bulimia

My question to you is, who were you before the bulimia started? Your answer might be, "I can't remember." Arrharr, but remember, there's always part of you that does know the answer! Your unconscious mind knows who you were before this behavior started, so ask it now:

"Who was I before the bulimia started?"

And you'll find that the first answer that comes into your head right now is the correct answer, directly from your unconscious mind.

I'm reasonably sure you weren't a serial killer or something much worse. You were just YOU, without the negative learnings, patterns, and behaviors. Just fabulous YOU.

You might be thinking, *But this is the only way I know how to cope right now*, and yes, I get that. But you could always begin to open the door to let a little light or a little willingness in. And make one small change in your life, one small step to moving forward to more light in your life.

Imagine what life would be like if you opened that door slightly now? To be honest, it's not going to kill you. It's going to allow you to see that you can begin to change. It's about making that decision to do it now.

 Complete the I'M SCARED OF WHO I AM WITHOUT BULIMIA table in Step 8, in your workbook. Otherwise, grab your notebook and ask yourself this question:

What specifically are you scared of if you no longer had bulimia?

You know what to do.

Tap on, for example:

"Even though I'm scared of who I am without bulimia, I deeply accept myself."

"Even though I may not like myself without bulimia, I deeply accept myself."

5. I'm scared of putting on weight.

Step 6, is all about the worries of putting weight on. So pop back and read this step to help you to understand further that while this may happen, it's only TEMPORARY. It won't last forever. Your weight will lessen.

It's your body adjusting to being fed and watered. You're just like a wilting flower. Providing food and water, you'll flourish into the blossoming beauty you were before the bulimia grabbed hold.

Imagine you've been in the garden and cut some beautiful pink roses. And you forgot to put them in water. Hours later, you remember, only to find wilting, tired, withering faded pink roses. Cutting the ends, you pop them in a vase of fresh water and nutrients. Within a couple of hours, your withering roses are a vibrant pink, sturdy, blooming beauties.

This will be once you start to change and focus on your eating plan. You too will be like a glorious, pink, energized, refreshed, new stunning rose.

By now, you'll be getting good at tapping and tuning in to what thoughts and feelings you're having.

 Complete the I'M SCARED OF PUTTING ON WEIGHT table in Step 8, in your workbook. Otherwise, grab your notebook and ask yourself this question:

What specifically are you scared of if you put weight on?

Work through your list, reducing what thoughts and feelings come up until you have each one down to a 0.

For example:

"Even though I'm scared to put weight on when I start on my structured eating program, I deeply accept myself."

"Even though I might not stop putting on weight when I start eating again, I deeply accept myself." (Remember what you learned about your body's natural set point; if you don't, then hop back to Step 6, and reread).

6.   I'm scared that the weight gain will be too fast?

Yes, this is a concern for all my clients in recovery but reread Step 6 again. If you do put weight on quickly, this will more likely be due to "the bulimia bloat" and will only be temporary. Your body isn't used to having food, so it may take time to adjust, but it will.

You can do this and deserve to live your life without bulimia.

Complete the I'M SCARED THAT THE WEIGHT GAIN WILL BE TOO FAST table in Step 8, in your workbook. Otherwise, grab your notebook and ask yourself this question:

Tap on your worry of fast weight gain after asking yourself:

What specifically are you scared of, if you were to put on weight quickly?

Make your list, then start tapping.

For example:

"Even though I'm scared my weight gain will be too fast, I deeply accept myself."

"Even though I might not lose the weight I put on, I deeply accept myself."

"ITS TIME TO CULTIVATE THAT SEED AND TO CONTROL THAT NEED!"

7. I'm scared if I do start eating, I'll never stop

I think you probably know the answer to this already. It will lead you into a binge. If that were to happen, that's okay. That's what recovery is all about. Three or four steps forward and one step back to start with, or maybe not.

If this were to happen, don't beat yourself up. So be it! You can choose to let it go. Then figure out what you can learn from it. And, more importantly, what you can do differently next time.

Complete the I'M SCARED IF I DO START EATING, I'LL NEVER STOP table in Step 8, in your workbook. Otherwise, grab your notebook and ask yourself this question:

What specifically are you scared of if you don't stop eating?

For example:

"Even though when I start eating, I might never stop, I deeply accept myself."

"Even though I might binge and purge and feel a failure if I can't stop eating, I deeply accept myself."

Again, if you aren't sure what you're scared of, if you lose control, tap on this.

"Even though I don't know why I'm scared if I do start eating and never stop, I deeply accept myself."

Then ask yourself the original question and tap on what comes up.

Fantastic, keep tap tap tapping on all your destructive thoughts and feelings.

WHAT'S FAILURE?

This may be a surprise, but there's no such thing! In the dictionary, failure means not being able to do something. It's just something negative you've done that you don't want.

It doesn't mean anything else but that! It doesn't mean you're hopeless or worthless. It's just an outcome of what you've done. That's all.

Oh yes, you may raise your eyebrows here, but it's true, failure is your approach, your mindset, your feeling you have, not a conclusion or an outcome. It's not to do with what you've done. It's the way you've been going about it.

That's what failure is all about. If we didn't fail, we wouldn't learn. We would be trapped in the same old place.

A failure is an event, not a person!

"THERE IS NO SUCH THING AS FAILURE
THERE ARE ONLY RESULTS WE CAN LEARN FROM"

Everyone has failures in their life.

Even Colonel Sanders failed 1,009 times!

Colonel Sanders, the creator of the KFC chain, in his snazzy, clean, crisp white coat, dashing black tie, and walking cane, spent most of his life working as a manager of a restaurant. After he retired, he started going door to door selling his secret fried chicken recipe. And it took him 1,009 "nos" before he finally got his first "yes" and then went on to build his global fried chicken empire.

He is an incredible inspiration to us all. He showed us that if we persevere, we can achieve whatever we want to. He found a way that would work for him; he found a way to use this challenge to keep him motivated.

I know this example is extreme. But it shows us that the way we think, talk to ourselves, and question ourselves holds us back.

As Thomas Edison said, "I haven't failed, I have just found 10,000 ways that don't work."

When we're trying to stop the urge to binge and fail, it makes us feel bad. We then question if we can ever overcome the claws of what we do. What this is telling us is that what we're doing now isn't working, so rethink and do something different.

ALEXA PENAVEGA - AMERICAN ACTRESS

After experiencing childhood in the spotlight, Pena Vega developed bulimia in response to a movie producer telling her she was too fat. For six years, she struggled to overcome the disease. "You read information. 'This is how you get over bulimia.' But it is so much deeper than that," she said. "I wish I'd had somebody who could have told me, 'It's scary.' You struggle, giving it up. You want to get rid of it, but you struggle because, in a strange way, you enjoy it" (Pearl, 2020).

STEP 8 - HERE ARE YOUR KEY EMPOWERING ACTION STEPS:

Start to push open that squeaky old door, let in a little light, have a peek. You may be surprised at the warmth and happiness the light brings you by taking that first empowering step toward living your life without bulimia.

- Where are your scared feelings now? Are they still lurking? If they are, it's time to tap tap tap.
- As you become more aware of what's genuinely scaring you, continue tapping on whatever negative thoughts or feelings that may arise.
- Enjoying the huge benefits as the feelings begin to lessen, opening up for more positive feelings. It will help guide and motivate you to continue working through other thoughts and feelings that come up.
- Each day, I want you to spend at least 15 minutes (more would be so much more beneficial!) tapping through your list of negative behaviors and then moving on to feelings, emotions, thoughts, urges.
- Failure - if we learn from our failure, we can feel positive about this, as it's going to lead us on a path that's simpler and easier.
- Where's your motivation to continue changing positively? If it's not fired up, then use your finger and thumb to power you up to move on to Step 9. An alternative would be to tap on it... Free yourself of any blockages and leap forward.

Your freedom may be scary because it's unknown, but it could also be exciting.

Now is the time to start to trust you're worth fighting for. You deserve a happy life, and it may be easier than you think.

STEP 9

WHAT THERAPIES CAN HELP ME?

"DON'T JUST GO THROUGH LIFE; IT'S NOW TIME TO GROW THROUGH INTO YOUR LIFE. BECOME THE SEED THAT FLOURISHES" —KATE HUDSON-HALL

Your empowering learnings from Step 8:

- You learned from Step 8 how your scared feelings could be part of what's stopping you from making changes in your behavior. And you've begun using your new EFT tapping technique on your fearful, scared, panicky feelings, clearing your mind to think about what your first step to change would be.

  You're making a list of these throughout your day and taking 15 minutes each day to work through your list, making sure each time you get that feeling down to a 0.

- Plus, when new habits arise, continue to break your habits instantly with the "Shatter That Habit" technique from Step 7.

The positive guidance you'll be learning here in Step 9:

- Learning about the different therapies that you could investigate to give you further support to help you through your recovery process.
- Understanding how you are going to learn from your "slip-ups." Plus, what you can do to bring yourself back on track to your recovery.
- Understand the importance of having the correct support for you to help you through your recovery journey.

Let's get motivated to move on to Step 9 and use your motivational anchor, pressing your finger and thumb together briefly imagine how you're going to be in the future, free from bulimia forever. Feel that motivation spreading over your whole body. Yeah, here we go...

"IT'S NEVER TO LATE TO TAKE ANOTHER PATH" —DAVID SUZUKI

WHAT THERAPIES CAN HELP ME?

There's a wide variety of therapies out there that can help you, but it's all about finding the right one that works for you.

Treatment for bulimia is most effective when it focuses, not so much on the eating behavior, although this is important, but on various areas like:

- Past events that could have triggered or influenced your relationship with food.
- Depression, anger, and failure.
- Reducing anxiety and stresses of life.
- Exploring the connection between emotions and eating.

- Addressing the idea that self-worth is based on weight.
- The causes of your behaviors. One may be a negative self-image that could have been created by a specific traumatic event or memory from your past.
- Working with your self-esteem and poor self-image. Identifying and changing limiting beliefs about your weight, dieting, and body shape.

A multi-directional approach is often best when treating bulimia, anorexia, or any eating disorder.

SUGGESTIONS FOR THERAPIES THAT COULD HELP YOU:

Psychotherapy

Psychotherapy also is known as talking therapy or psychological counseling. It's the most common treatment for bulimia. Much research has been done to support how beneficial psychotherapy is to help people begin to address all the areas surrounding their bulimia.

Talking through a problem helps to gain an understanding of how and why the problem exists and strategize new ways of responding differently to a specific difficulty. There are many different types of talking therapies that you could investigate to help you overcome your bulimia. I wanted to give an overview of how it will help you and some of the different types.

A therapist's primary goal is to help you learn about you and recognize and turn toward your problem, giving you the tools to feel more confident and deal with stressful situations. Your therapist will also help you explore other areas of your life associated with your bulimia - for example, sexual abuse, anxiety, and depression.

Cognitive–Behavioural Therapy (CBT)

This is a fantastic form of psychotherapy treatment to guide you in your understanding between your thoughts, feeling, and actions. By recognizing how you create this specific behavior, you can learn from it and change your behavior.

CBT will also help to work with your negative feelings and behaviors such as food restriction and your urge to binge cycle, address your eating patterns, and identify unhealthy, negative beliefs and behaviors and replace them with healthy, positive ones.

Research from Washington University School of Medicine, St. Louis, Missouri, USA. Denise E. Wilfley, Ph.D. finds cognitive-behavioral therapy (CBT) and interpersonal psychotherapy (IPT) remains the most established treatments for bulimia nervosa and binge eating disorder, with stepped-care approaches showing promise and new behavioral treatments under study (Kass, Kolko, & Wilfley, 2013).

Hypnotherapy

One of the therapies I believe genuinely helped me to overcome my bulimia was hypnotherapy. As I said, this was one of the reasons I decided to train as a psychotherapist and hypnotherapist, without either of these therapies, who knows where I would be today. I probably would still have the ugly green leprechaun torment me.

Let me begin by explaining that hypnotherapy utilizes the heightened awareness of the hypnotic state to help you explore your bulimia more deeply.

So, what is hypnosis?

Hypnosis is a relaxation technique. Many of my clients think it's going to be something very "out there." But it's just like relaxing in a chair!

As you're guided into a relaxing, calm trance state, you're more open to suggestions. It's very much like daydreaming. For example, have you ever been watching TV, and someone has been talking to you, but you've been so focused on your TV show that you don't hear what they're saying? This is a form of trance.

Hypnotherapy is similar to these experiences, except that this altered state of consciousness is used to implement positive change. Under hypnosis, you remain conscious and in control. But you're relaxed and highly focused. Your mind is highly responsive to any suggestions given. That's why it's so powerful to help work with negative thoughts and feelings connected with your bulimia.

It's working with the root causes of these actions, habits, and patterns with the unconscious with suggestions to improve and enhance how the unconscious operates, therefore, changing the behaviors positively.

How does it feel to be in a trance?

Being in a trance is my favorite place to be! It's a relaxed and natural state to experience. Some people may experience a feeling of heaviness or a floating sensation. It's just like being in that stage just before you go to sleep or awaken in the morning when you can still hear what's going on, but you're drifting.

In Step 1, you learned the differences between your conscious and your unconscious mind. Hypnotherapy will assist you in breaking the cycle of bulimia by working with both the conscious and unconscious mind.

You'll learn to think differently and open the doors to flexibility in your feelings and thoughts and assist you in making positive, conscious choices.

As I mentioned, for me, hypnotherapy was one of the keys to me breaking free from the chains of bulimia, uncovering many of the negative thought patterns and behaviors that cemented the path of my bulimia, guiding me forward with the tools and strength and empowerment to heal.

I remember feeling trapped in the cycle of bingeing and purging, but hypnotherapy helped to reprogram my mind, to replace the old cycle of thinking and behavior and improving my relationship with food and myself.

 I have had powerful experiences of positive change with hypnotherapy. Once I trained as a hypnotherapist, I worked successfully with many clients with bulimia, anorexia, and binge eating disorders. It's a fantastic therapy to help free the unconscious negative patterns and connections.

Neuro Linguist Programming (NLP)

NLP was developed by two incredible minds, John Grinder and Richard Bandler, at the University of California in Santa Cruz in the early 1970s. It's such an incredibly powerful change therapy, using different techniques to overcome negative thoughts and feelings while reprogramming your mind to think positively. I learned NLP two decades ago and have modified these methods to precisely help my clients with bulimia, anorexia, and other eating disorders.

You've already learned so much about NLP throughout this book. Similar to hypnosis, it works with your unconscious mind. Reprogramming it to achieve what you want in life free from bulimia consciously.

 Your bulimia with NLP techniques rapidly replaces painful feelings with feelings of positivity. NLP is focusing on a 90% solution of what you want, how you want to be in the future, rather than on the specific problem.

Mindfulness

Mindfulness is a specific way of paying attention to whatever is happening in your life right now, here, in the present moment, as you're probably, like all us, thinking about the past or worrying or planning for the future.

You may be wondering why it's so important to be in the present moment. But considerable research has been done on the incredible benefits and essential changes that happen to the brain when we practice mindfulness. Your brain is effectively rewiring and helping you to recognize and begin changing habits, unconscious emotions, and psychological reactions to what you do each day.

In Step 3, you learned what mindfulness is and how to use it with your urges and your new skill of "Urge Surfing."

It's time to practice mindfulness. By introducing it into your everyday life, it will help you to become more aware of that toxic leprechaun chatter and bring you back to the present moment. It will give you a huge break. It's like pressing the pause button of your busy mind and giving yourself a complete break from all that thinking. Now, who wouldn't want that!

Family Therapy

Family Therapy is an excellent way for you, your parents and siblings to explore how your bulimia is affecting your relationships. As often, family members have strong feelings of guilt and anxiety. Your family dynamics that may be intensifying your behaviors or disrupting your recovery need to be addressed.

Family Therapy involves learning together to improve communication and how family members can support you in your recovery.

Nutrition Counseling

The main goal of a nutritionist or a dietician is to guide you into healthy eating behaviors and introducing them into your everyday life. They will help you develop a healthier relationship with food. Wow! How amazing would it be to look forward to eating for the pleasure of it rather than trying to change your feelings?

Group Therapy

Anorexic and Bulimics Anonymous (ABA)

This is a self-supporting group which includes the twelve-step program adapted from Alcoholic Anonymous to address the mental, emotional, and spiritual components of anorexia and bulimia.

By following the twelve steps, it's about coming to a deep level of freedom from obsessions with your body, shape, and food. Learning that eating disorders are a form of addiction, and the key to recovery is finding sobriety in eating and exercise patterns.

For that support and guidance to your freedom, research the many therapies out there, and find the right one for you.

"EVERY PATH HAS ITS PUDDLE" —ENGLISH PROVERB

RELAPSE

A relapse is a reoccurring event to a binge or purge. It's reverting into your old habits and patterns, obsessing about your weight, listening to that devious leprechaun's nonsense chatter about your weight, self-image, and food.

RELAPSE OR SLIP UP?

The word "relapse" is implying that this could happen again. It's telling that unconscious part of your brain that you'll do it again! Which is quite the opposite of where we're going with your new positive focus of change.

First, I think you should change the word from relapse to "SLIP-UP," as a "slip" means "to slide," and it's okay to slide; it's temporarily losing your hold or footing. "Up" implies that yes, you've slipped, but you're already on the up, getting your focus back.

WHAT IF I SLIP UP?

You're durable, just like a battery!

So, you may have slip-ups when that urge or drive to binge is just too overwhelming, which can be discouraging. But then, you may not as you begin to change your patterns. But if you were to have a slip-up, which happens sometimes, it doesn't mean that you're failing because it's a normal part of recovery.

 The most exciting part is that you can learn from your slip-up. You become more understanding of yourself and so much more durable because you choose to keep focused on your end goal of breaking free from bulimia each time. You pick yourself up, brush yourself off, and begin again. Each time you do this, you're proving to your bulimia just how resilient you are and solidifying your foundation to make your recovery permanent.

FAILURE ISN'T THE END OF THE ROAD. IT'S A BIG RED FLAG SAYING TO YOU, 'WRONG WAY. TURN AROUND' —OPRAH WINFREY

Do your red flags blindly flap in the wind?

A hugely crucial and vital part of your recovery is to be aware of your specific potential red flags or your warning signs. These can vary greatly. So, it's imperative to tune in to your patterns of what you're thinking and feeling. Become aware of yourself starting to:

- Obsess about your weight
- Skip meals

- Maybe see your old negative beliefs slithering in, like not being good enough, worthlessness, helplessness

 As you make all these positive changes in your life, you'll start to feel all your emotions again, both pleasant and unpleasant. So, it's learning to identify the specifically difficult ones. Then use the tools you've learned in this book to understand from them and work through them.

But after following the program, you'll find it easier to identify accurately what your potential red flags could be if that were to happen.

It's about being aware of these and then figuring out what you're going to do differently.

What can I do differently if I do slip up?

There are many avenues to take if this were to happen, for example:

 1.   Be kind to yourself; it's not going to help if you beat yourself up over this.

2.   Being aware of your negative thoughts connected with your slip-up and practice your thought-stopping technique in Step 5, which you'll have been using, to distance yourself from the devious leprechaun sitting on your shoulder.

3.   I want you to take out your notes and step into that "new you" technique from Step 1 and really feel what your future has to hold free from bulimia.

4.   Tap Tap Tap. Yes, it's time to tap, tune in to the negative thoughts, the negative feelings, and start to tap on everything that comes up connected to your slip-up, working through and reducing them down to a 0.

For example:

   o   "Even though I feel guilty or disappointed that I've had a slip-up, I deeply and completely accept myself."

   o   "Even though I'm ashamed and angry with myself, I deeply and completely accept myself."

5.   Tuning in to what happened earlier rather than later when you know you're headed down that dangerous road is crucial to your learning and recovery.

 6.   Complete the 'SLIP UP' table in Step 9, in your workbook. Otherwise, grab your notebook and make a list of where you think you took that first step onto the slip. What were you thinking and feeling? Had something upsetting just happened? Make a list of what you could do differently if it were to happen again.

"There are no failures—only feedback" —Richard Bandler

"INSPIRE YOUR SMOLDERING FIRE" TECHNIQUE

This is a technique for you to learn and use anytime you may not feel too confident about the enormous changes you'll be making. So, let's learn how you can pump up positive feelings anytime you wish.

I can do it; you can do it. We all can do it!

- Close your eyes and imagine a big movie screen right in front of you; you can see yourself, thoughts, and feelings. There's a big old-fashioned lever connected to what you see on the screen.
- Go Back in your mind to a really good experience when you felt super positive, having achieved something that made you proud. Feel what you felt then.
- Picture the image getting bigger and closer and more vivid as the positive feelings increase. Imagine the lever has a label on it that says, "I can do this," and slowly move it up. To make it feel more real, bring the lever up.
- As you slide it up at the rate that fits the changes in your psychology and feelings. Allow that exhilarating positive memory to get closer and closer and bigger and brighter. Add color to it. Make it shine and look at all the details. Hear a voice in your head that says, "I can do this." Enjoy this incredible sensation for a moment or two. Then pull the lever down to the initial position and let your body return to a more neutral state.
- Now check if the anchoring was successful. Stop for a moment and then grab the lever again, turning it up as you say to yourself, "I can do this." You should go back to feeling as ecstatic as before.

 Great, I want you to keep pumping up the volume when you aren't feeling positive about your recovery. Keep jumping into the image and telling yourself you can do this; you can change (Bandler, Roberti, & Fitzpatrick, 2013).

Video Demonstration Link: https: //bulimiasucks.com/inspire-your-smoldering-fire/

**"THERE ARE NO WRONG TURNS,
ONLY UNEXPECTED PATHS"** —Mark Nepo

RECOMMENDED SUPPLEMENTS

Due to malnutrition, clients with bulimia are much more likely to suffer from vitamin and mineral deficiencies. Visiting a nutritionist would be hugely beneficial in your recovery.

Probiotics

Even before visiting a nutritionist, it would be a great idea to start taking probiotics. These live bacteria help restore the natural balance of bacteria in your gut (including your stomach and intestines). Within these, there are good and bad bacteria; people with bulimia may have a low number of good bacteria.

It would be beneficial to begin taking probiotics to build on the good bacteria and reduce gases and cravings of carbohydrates and sugar caused by the harmful bacteria. You can get probiotics from supplements as well as from foods such as yogurts.

Here are further supplements you may wish to add to your meal plan, although consult your doctor or nutritionist before doing so:

A daily multivitamin

Many people feel the benefits by taking a high-quality daily multivitamin containing the antioxidant vitamins A, B, C, and E, vitamins, and trace minerals such as magnesium, calcium, zinc, phosphorus, and copper. Make sure the multivitamin has a balance B complex. This is useful in helping the body cope with stress.

Zinc

One five-year study showed an astounding 85% recovery rate from bulimia in patients given zinc supplementation. It concluded that zinc supplementation resulted in weight restoration, better body function, and improved outlook.

Omega-3 oils

Omega-3 is not only good for helping ease anxiety and stress but also has many other reported health benefits such as lowering blood pressure and possibly reducing the risk of coronary heart disease.

Calcium

Most bulimics are low in calcium, which is essential for healthy bones and teeth. It would be a good idea to increase your calcium consumption through supplements and with vitamin D (which helps the absorption of the calcium) and in your structured eating program, such as cabbage, spinach, and broccoli, and then with calcium supplements.

Magnesium

This is an electrolyte that's essential for maintaining a healthy heart. Taking magnesium supplements are great for muscle tension, insomnia, and heart palpitations.

Potassium

Most bulimics are deficient in potassium, which is essential for the correct functioning of the heart, kidneys, muscles, nerves, and digestive system. Therefore, potassium supplements would be beneficial to investigate. In your structured eating program, increase foods high in potassium such as bananas, oranges, apricots, avocado, potatoes, tomatoes, cucumber, cabbage, tuna, beef, chicken, sardines, and salmon.

REACH OUT FOR SUPPORT

Many of my clients with bulimia have suffered for years silently and totally alone. Telling someone that they have bulimia requires enormous courage and can be daunting. Opening up about their intensely private struggle means facing anxieties and fears.

They fear that the person they've chosen to tell will be uncomfortable if they knew the truth, when in fact, if they're living with the person, they probably have an inkling.

When you're ready to open up and share your deepest secrets, it can feel very intimidating to begin with, but you'll feel incredibly empowered afterward.

Think about if your friend came to you to tell you a deep dark secret, how would you react? Would you feel burdened by their issue? NO, you would be very compassionate and do whatever you could to support them.

Statistics show the vast majority of people with eating disorders either never seek formal treatment or are never formally diagnosed.

People with bulimia are often of 'normal' weight

Yes, people with bulimia are frequently of 'normal' weight, compared with anorexics who are usually underweight. Which can cause difficulties in its own right as:

- When they are ready to reach out for help, sometimes they are not believed. I know this is shocking, but it's true. But if this may be the case, they weren't the right person to tell; but stay focused and find someone else!
- It makes it easier to successfully hide their bulimic problem; therefore, loved ones may be less aware of their difficulties.

Statistics show that approximately 80% of people with an eating disorder are not underweight.

How to tell someone you have bulimia

Who in your life, friend or family member, do you fully trust and can 100% rely on?

Four main points to focus on when telling your chosen friend or family member about your bulimia:

- Tell them in private when they're not distracted.
- Be honest with them and yourself.
- Be understanding of their reaction, although it's more than likely to be compassion. Most of my clients find that sharing their secrets and reaching for help brings them much closer to that individual than they have ever been.
- Explain to them how they can support you.

The more people you have to support you during your recovery, the more positive you'll feel, and the more relaxed your recovery will be.

Bulimia can be painfully lonely, so come and join us on our Facebook page, "Bulimia Sucks!" at https://www.facebook.com/groups/BulimiaSuck/. It can be encouraging to connect with others who are going through the same experiences as you and to hear how they've overcome specific problems in their recovery.

GERI HALLIWELL (SINGER)

Ginger Spice admitted that she became "locked in a cycle of 'comfort eating and purging.' For me, [it] was controlling my body weight." That obsession and desire to control showed itself in strict dieting and exercise, emotional eating, and issues with bulimia. Even worse, it was a battle Halliwell's fellow spice girls were completely unaware of. "I started being bulimic, and no one would notice it because your body weight stays pretty much the same. It's bloody dangerous," she explained. "I was worried I'd get fat. I would binge and then felt fatter and would make myself sick, it was awful." She says on her recovery: "Step by step, the road is long, but at the end, you can touch a star" (Brown West-Rosenthal, 2016).

STEP 9 - HERE ARE YOUR KEY EMPOWERING ACTION STEPS:

- Having read about all the incredible therapies that could help you to move forward, depending on where you are in your recovery, choose one that you think will help you immensely and get proactive.

Research on the internet for more information.

Find a group online (as there are plenty).

Call a few local eating disorder-specific therapists or nutritionists to find out more information.

Visit my website: bulimiasucks.com

Join our Bulimia Sucks! Facebook page: https://www. facebook.com/groups/BulimiaSuck/ for further help and motivation to take you forward.

- If you have slip-ups, it doesn't mean you're failing because it's a normal part of recovery. Learn from them for next time you're in the same situation. Follow a different path.
- Where are your scared feelings now? Are they still lurking? If they are, it's time to tap, tap, tap, and just keep tapping on any negativity that may come up.

You're an incredible, strong being, whether you feel and see that right now or not. You have the inner strength within you to free you of bulimia. Believe you can, and you're halfway there.

STEP 10

EMPOWERING TOP TIPS TO GUIDE YOU FURTHER IN YOUR RECOVERY.

"Rock bottom became the solid foundation on which I rebuilt my life" —J K Rowling

THIS STEP IS ALL ABOUT YOU, YOU, AND MORE IMPORTANTLY... YOU

Imagine you're a student of Hogwarts and have a magic wand gripped in your hand. If you were to wave that magic wand and it could grant you one wish that would give you the courage, motivation, and inspiration to change and take that first step to freedom from bulimia...

Complete the ONE WISH TO FREEDOM table in Step 10, in your workbook. Otherwise, grab your notebook and answer these questions:

Ask yourself:	Your answers:

What would that wish be?

What's stopping you?

What techniques can you   List the specific techniques

use to reduce the blockages

that are stopping you from

starting?

OOMPH, you did it... Now start to implement your first step toward your wish. Having read through the book and from all you have learned, you'll begin to see and feel that you do have a choice, and choice is power.

Your empowering learnings from Step 9:

- Having learned about some therapies that could help you in your recovery, now take some time out and do some research. Having the right support in your recovery will be immensely empowering to help and guide you toward your light.
- Use this book to educate your loved ones on bulimia, have them read the free family support handout at the end of the book. Add to this anything that they could do to help you.
- From what you've learned about slip-ups, remind yourself that they're a normal part of recovery and learn from them.

- Having discovered your tapping skills, continue to tap on any painful feeling that springs to the surface, or just tap tap tap on that evil leprechaun's gibberish.
- Keep running your "Inspire Your Smoldering Fire" technique because you can do it and have that ecstatic feeling rise as you lift that lever whenever you're feeling wobbly about your recovery.

The positive guidance you'll be learning here in Step 10:

- An excellent clear recovery action plan (Yes, you need to have a vision of how you're going to move forward healthily)
- Understand the importance of
    - Having a goal to work toward and how to make exciting empowering ones
    - Plus, visualizing your end goal when you're fully recovered and leading a normal life like everyone else
- How you're going to address that stress
- Learn a fantastic technique to power up your motivation to change
- Understand what's going to happen in the months after you've made that decision to begin your recovery process

10 TOP TIPS ON HOW TO ELECTRIFY YOUR LIGHTBULB MOMENTS

Here, you're going to learn the extra top tips that are going to support you in your change right now.

1. WHEN IS THE RIGHT TIME TO START YOUR RECOVERY?

Let's think about when the right time to start your recovery would be. Maybe tomorrow or next week or after some big event in your life? ERRRR NO! **NOWWWWWWWW**, it's undeniably, right NOW. The good news is you don't need to wait until you feel 100% ready to start recovery! Because let's be honest, that will probably be never!

What would happen if you decided here and now that you were going to take your leprechaun by the horns and begin to address all his negative babbling connected to your thinking, feelings, your triggers, and urges that cause your bingeing and purging?

What could be the worst thing that's going to happen to you? Let me tell you, NOTHING, just an improvement in your health.

**SO, ARE YOU READY TO SPRING OFF
THAT MERRY-GO-ROUND AND FLIP THAT SPIKY
LEPRECHAUN'S HORNS INTO OBLIVION?**

Make the decision

This may not be an easy decision to make, but the sooner you begin looking at and addressing your behaviors, the faster you'll recover.

Yes, you might have slips and slides, and that's to be expected, but it's staying focused on your decision; think about how you'll be in 3 months from now. How much healthier you'll look, think, and feel, how proud you'll be of yourself.

YES, COME ON... YOU CAN DO THIS...

2. CREATE A VISION

You need to have a vision, a picture, an image of where you're going with your recovery, how you're going to change when you've achieved that 3-month goal and live it in your mind.

Use your new toolbox of submodalities from Step 1, and the "A New You" technique. Create an image of how you would like to look, think, and feel in 3 months to truly empower you to feel excited and motivated to take action. By reinforcing your positive self-image with powerful, positive feelings, you start to teach your brain that you want to change.

What image are you creating? Make it bigger, brighter, super colorful, as if it's the most empowering image you've ever seen. BOOM! Jump into that image and feel that energizing inspiration rising as the excitement of change engulfs you.

This is what'll give you the drive to stay focused. You'll feel so much more durable; you'll feel amazing, healthier, and have more energy.

Visualize your positive recovery

Once you've made it to the 3-month mark, then focus on your recovery for the next 3 months. Look at what you need to change or do differently, maybe nothing. But imagine this in great detail.

Taking it day by day, week by week, month by month. Studies show people recovering from bulimia once they reach that 6-month goal then motivates them to continue until they're entirely free from bulimia.

Once you've achieved your 6-month goal and stopped celebrating, then focus on the next 3 months, step by step.

HOW TO STAY MOTIVATED: "TAKE IT ONE STEP AT A TIME, SURROUND YOURSELF WITH POSITIVITY, CREATE A VISION, MAKE ACHIEVABLE GOALS, REWARD YOURSELF, BELIEVE IN YOURSELF" —KATE HUDSON-HALL

3. GOAL SETTING

LET'S LEARN ABOUT THE IMPORTANCE OF SETTING YOUR GOALS TO PROPEL YOU INTO YOUR POSITIVE FUTURE

Now that you have your vision, you're going to incorporate this within your goal-setting plans.

WHAT IS GOAL SETTING?

Goal setting allows you to take control of your life's direction. It provides you with a gauge for determining how you're doing and if you're actually moving forward in your recovery and succeeding.

Many people don't realize how powerful making goals are. But by focusing consistently, your goal will become real, and you'll experience it.

Some of my clients, when first coming to see me, look at their recovery path as a painful struggle. Yes, it may not be so easy; there will be bumps in your path and you may even veer off. But it's about becoming aware that's where you are and hoisting yourself back to your constructive pathway, using the techniques in this book. And create inspiring motivating goals for all the incredible changes you'll be making.

Goal setting and working with your conscious and unconscious mind.

- By setting your goals, you're working not only with your conscious mind but also with your unconscious mind. The goals you make will highlight to your conscious and unconscious mind where you are now, and this creates dissatisfaction in your brain, which will give you the power to drive your motivation to begin changing your life.

Empowering goals propel you forward?

We all have goals throughout our day, whether that's making yourself a cup of coffee, taking a shower, getting the kids ready and off to school, doing your washing. The problem is they don't exactly inspire that excitement within you. No flame would explode into exhilaration to move forward in life.

The key to setting great goals is to make them as empowering as possible. Imagine throwing petrol on a dying, smoldering bonfire; it suddenly erupts into a dynamic explosion of excitement. This is what you want to achieve when you decide on your goals to encourage you to grow and flourish, to feel that bonfire erupt inside you. Yes, this is how I want you to feel when you set your goals.

I saw an interview with someone who has known Boris Johnson, our UK Prime Minister, from a young age. He explained that when Boris was a very young boy, he decided he wanted to become King of the World; this was his goal. When he was ten, he decided maybe that wasn't such a clear goal and decided, instead, to become the UK Prime Minister. Eventually, in his 50s, he achieved it.

Whether you're a supporter of Boris or not, this is a perfect example of goal setting; he had the vision and determination to achieve.

Time for you to make your own goals

Make your goals achievable.

Recovery can be scary and not easy, so it's incredibly important to set achievable goals yourself. Many people set unrealistic goals, which they're unable to achieve. Of course, this creates many negative thoughts and feelings about themselves, which could trigger that leprechaun to spring back into action, something we want to avoid.

Write your goals.

 Complete the GOALS table in Step 10, in your workbook. Otherwise, grab your notebook, and you're going to use your old skill in writing, which is something many of us don't do anymore.

Stay clear of jumping on your computer and typing them. Studies show that by actually writing down your goals, you're accessing both the left and right hemispheres of your brain. You're opening up the unconscious mind to seeing opportunities that can't be detected if you're just typing them while thinking about them. By literally writing down your goals, it transforms your thoughts into reality.

It's time to break down the details of your goals.

Make clear, specific goals.

Goal setting is about making clear, detailed goals. Most people, when they create goals, don't have a particular, clear vision of where they're going.

The more specific you can be when making your goals, the more powerful they become.

It's not just about deciding how you want to be in the future and then bumbling your way toward that. It's breaking down the specific steps of how you're going to get there, giving you direction of how you're going to achieve your outcome. Without goals, you lack focus and direction.

Say you had created a goal for the week: "My goal for the week is I mustn't binge and purge."

One crucial point I want to remind you of from Step 1 is that when setting your goals, be aware of how you specifically word them. Remember to word it in the positive. Your unconscious mind doesn't hear any negative words said to it. Therefore, it doesn't hear the word "mustn't." Thus, in effect, you're saying your goal is that you must binge and purge.

 Hot Tip—Don't *listen to everything I tell you in the book!* Get what I mean? OK, maybe not, if you have missed what I said earlier, so let me repeat it: YOUR UNCONSCIOUS MIND DOESN'T HEAR ANY NEGATIVE WORDS SAID TO IT, So, wording your goals in the positive is essential. Therefore:

Hot Tip—~~Don't~~ listen to everything I tell you in the book!

Words to avoid are: Can't, won't, don't, mustn't, not, and never.

It's about learning to word it in the positive, giving your unconscious mind obvious direction. Instead, you could say:

"My goal for the week is to eat one of my three meals a day calmly, to nourish my body."

Although they both virtually mean the same thing, our subconscious mind reads them entirely differently.

 Complete the POWERFUL POSITIVE GOALS table in Step 10, in your workbook. Otherwise, grab your notebook and make a list now of three positive goals you're going to achieve this week. Review this each week and change your goals.

1.

2.

3.

Repeat, repeat, repeat

The power comes from repetition. You have to keep repeating your new skills and goals to get what you want. Through repetition, your new skill can become a new habit and make that profound and lasting impact on you and your future.

"YOUR DIDN'T COME THIS FAR TO ONLY COME THIS FAR"

4. YOUR RECOVERY ACTION PLAN

Your recovery isn't about giving anything up; it's gaining knowledge and understanding. This is so exciting; your pathway through recovery will bring hundreds of new revelations every day. You may even find you like some of them that you never knew you had, tucked away in your bottom draws.

YOU TOO CAN CHANGE... NOW

Many of my recovered clients say they can't remember what it feels like to be bulimic. They've changed in so many ways:

- they no longer have urges to binge and purge.
- their brain chemistry has changed, and food is to be eaten and enjoyed.
- their leprechaun has slipped into a dark hole, never to be seen again.

This may seem impossible to you right now, but this can and will happen to you once you make that decision now to change and follow each step in the book to freedom.

IT'S TIME TO MAKE A RECOVERY ACTION PLAN

It's time to incorporate all the advice, guidance, and learning you've read in this book and create your very own action plan.

In the table below, complete what you specifically need to change and then what you're going to do differently to help you make your action plan.

Complete the ACTION PLAN table in Step 10, in your workbook. Otherwise, grab your notebook and answer these questions:

WHAT SPECIFICALLY DO I NEED TO CHANGE?	WHAT AM I GOING TO DO DIFFERENTLY?
1.	
2.	
3.	
4.	
5.	

Your freedom is there waiting around the corner! You will regain not only your self-respect and confidence but also your unique dazzling sparkle and, most importantly, YOUR LIFE.

5. TECHNIQUE TIME

Now you have your list of what you need to change and do differently to keep yourself motivated and focused. Below is a list of all the incredible techniques you've learned in the book. I want you to work your way again through these, listing the changes you need to make as you move forward in your recovery and finding which techniques really fire up that motivation or help incredibly to change the way you feel in order to make that positive change. Then keep practicing these on a never-ending loop.

Complete the TECHNIQUE TIME table in Step 10, in your workbook. Otherwise, grab your notebook and make your list of changes based on this example:

TECHNIQUE   **LIST CHANGES TO MAKE**

"A NEW YOU"

"SHRINK & BLINK"

"INSTANT TRIGGER CHANGE"

"ELECTRIFY YOUR MOTIVATION"

"URGE SURFING"

"CHANGE YOUR BELIEFS INSTANTLY"

"THOUGHT STOPPING"

"SPIN & WIN"

"SHATTER THAT HABIT"

"EFT"

"INSPIRE YOUR SMOLDERING FIRE"

"MOTIVATION BOOSTER"

"LIFE IS 10% WHAT HAPPENS TO ME AND 90% OF HOW I REACT TO IT" —CHARLES SWINDOLL

6. WHAT ARE YOUR POWERFUL REASONS TO RECOVER FROM BULIMIA?

For years, many of my clients have struggled to find what will motivate them to recover from bulimia. When they don't find an answer, well, the easiest route to take is the familiar one, so the behavior has continued.

It's crucial to understand why you want to recover, and this compelling reason is usually something more important to you than your bulimia.

With my clients, there are usually three main reasons why they want to make that decision and start with their recovery process.

1. To follow a career or passion

Living with bulimia can absorb most of your thinking, so there isn't much time left for anything else, especially building your career or your own company. But once my clients have realized this is their life's goal, they have a strong reason to begin to step onto their recovery path.

2. Relationships

It's challenging to be in a long-term relationship when you already have a relationship with bulimia! It zaps all your energy. Often, that strong desire to be in a secure relationship and have children becomes much more compelling than bulimia.

3. Fun, Fun, Fun

Your bulimia has been standing in the way of you having any fun, which we all love to do at some level, whether that's enjoying the outdoors, reading, or traveling. What would it be for you?

You may have a hidden reason why you can't break free from bulimia. But your reason to choose recovery is lurking inside you; it's probably behind that spleen with its friends!

Are you ready...?

 Suppose you're ready to begin on your recovery path, Complete the RECOVERY PATH table in Step 10, in your workbook. Otherwise, grab your notebook and answer this question, then make your list:

"What would life look like if I didn't have bulimia?"

It could be learning to skydive or taking a course you have a passion for connected with a career, maybe?

From your answers, see if you can identify the reasons why you may *want to change.*

Understand why you want to stop this behavior. Then, once you're aware of this, you can clearly see what you're willing to do to stop your bulimia.

7. YOUR TIMELINE TO RECOVERY

Let's look at the breakdown of how you'll change over the next year in your incredibly liberating recovery process.

As you travel through your recovery, it's essential to keep in mind that everyone is different. The length of your recovery really depends on the severity of your bulimia, how many slip-ups you may have, and how quickly you work through each step and find what works for you. This could be anywhere between 6 to 18 months. So this is a rough guide.

Hang on...

Before you begin, go back to the beginning of this book, entirely focusing on following each step to completely understand where you are now and how you're going to learn to begin to break your old habits, behaviors, and patterns.

As you work through each critical day, your mind will begin to rewire and change as your body adjusts to your new eating patterns.

 Remember, day by day, you're climbing step by step out of your dark hole; maybe you can already see a spec of light at the top? Or perhaps it's still dark and dingy in there. However, right now, keep reminding yourself that you can change and break those chains of bulimia.

Now that you've learned the "Emotional Freedom Technique," tap on all the problematic thoughts and feelings you have about starting your recovery process. By reducing these stressful feelings, you'll feel even more motivated to begin.

LET'S LOOK WEEK BY WEEK, STEP BY STEP, WHAT WILL HAPPEN IN YOUR RECOVERY

Week 1

- Oh, these first few days, you may feel swamped with painful thoughts, feelings, and fears churning around, and you may well be drained, but this is a very normal part of recovery. It's expected.

It's your poisonous leprechaun, your bulimia voice that's saying, "Hey, you're no good; you can't do this; you're not good enough; you're hopeless, helpless, and worthless." He wants you to fall back into your old behaviors, but you must beat him off; he's toxic and cruel.

This is incredibly important that you hear and understand this. To dispel the beastly leprechaun, you can keep knocking him from your shoulder by using the "Thought Stopping" technique from Step 5, to begin to free you of his rantings. Also, tap on whatever comes up.

- As you learn more about you, many new positive revelations start to unfold, which inspires you to stay focused on your structured eating program.
- Your urges to binge and purge could increase; this is a regular occurrence.
- When you're ready, start to reduce the number of times per day you weigh yourself and gradually reduce this as the week progresses until you feel empowered to toss the scales in the bin, which is where they belong.

Be compassionate with yourself and give yourself a break; this is a substantial first milestone.

Week 2 to 3

- Your urges to binge and purge could continue to increase. So, start to become more aware of these and be kind and compassionate with yourself. Rather than trying not to think about the unbearable urge to binge or push it away, turn toward the urge; stay firmly with it.

  It's about getting to know it, sitting with it, and choosing to accept it and feel it. See how long you can sit with it, if only for 30 seconds, and if you do binge and purge, so be it, but what can you learn from it? Then build from there.

  You'll be surprised when, after turning toward the unbearable fearful feelings the urge is creating in you and accepting these feelings, they'll become less intense and loosen their grip on you. They'll begin to reduce and dissolve. This is the time to go back to Step 3, and learn to ride the urges with the "Urge Surfing" technique.

- As you start to eat more food, that dreaded bloating could well have slithered in. Reread Step 6, and learn how you can deal with any physical stomach pain and all these emotions; the more knowledgeable you are, the more comfortable you'll be dealing with what's happening to your mind and body.

  Keep using the "Spin to Win" technique. To beat this bloating beast, you have to keep eating and nourishing your body with adequate nutrients and sufficient calories. If you do start to bloat, remember to wear loose baggy clothing and keep reminding yourself this is temporary.

- Your triggers will be encouraging your devious leprechaun to yell even louder. But as you slowly become aware of your triggers, then you can make changes to them and begin to break that chain of events that lead you into bingeing and purging. Time to work with the Instant Trigger Change technique in Step 2.
- Exhaustion may increase, so go easy with it; you have a considerable amount of changes going on with your mind and body. As much as you can, take time out and focus on what you need to do to relax, sleep, recover, and heal.
- Your structured eating program will be continuing to develop into an excellent healthy routine, and you may have had half or one full day of following your eating plan without wobbling. If you have, oh my gosh, it's time to give yourself a huge pat on the back, your stomach, and anywhere else you want! Congratulations!

When you aren't feeling inspired to continue or have a slip-up, use your "Motivation Booster" technique to fire you up again, which you will be learning in this step.

Week 4 to 6

- You still have ups and maybe not so many down days. Your leprechaun again may spring into action, verbally attacking you. But at times when, in the past, he would typically be screaming, now he's not and this is lessening.

Fearful thoughts and feelings still swish into your urges, but the good news is that these are diminishing. But like a roller coaster, they can still build as you continue to urge surf with them.

- Your initial bloating will have decreased slightly. Wahooo! How exciting is that? But if it's still there, you're beginning to more clearly understand that it's just a temporary part of your recovery, and you're opening up to accept this. Because of this, you'll be feeling much more assured to continue with your recovery. Keep reminding yourself that the bulimia bloat is only temporary.

- You have learned now how important it is not to restrict your eating and continue with your tailored structured eating program. Now, maybe it's time to re-read Step 4, and begin with your intuitive eating plan.
- Only eating when you're hungry. Start to use the hunger scale to guide you.
- Slowly eat as you focus on the incredible tastes and flavors of your food.
- Tune in to your feelings of contentment or knowing when you've had enough and you're at that moderately full stage.
- Make a list of what's been working for you and keep using your tools and techniques to support you in your recovery.

Week 7 to 3 months

- There may still be days when you feel down and want to go back to restricting foods, but at this stage, most times, you get through it and stay focused. But your significant mood swings will have been reduced, and you'll be experiencing more stable emotions, therefore, having less anxiety.

Maybe you can see a flicker of light in the distance as you look toward the top of your dark hole.

- Begin to clearly see more of your old habits and spend time working with the Shatter That Habit technique from Step 7, to break these patterns.
- Bloating should be beginning to deflate. Your metabolism will have speeded up as it feels more confident that regular food will be coming; therefore, your weight will be settling down, although the bloating may come and go over the next few months. But it will settle down.
- Your structured eating will be so much more controllable. I'm not saying eating still isn't a struggle some days, but you'll be feeling calmer about it.
- As your confidence swells, your self-esteem will also grow.
- Sleeping will be improved at this stage; as you feel calmer, the quality of sleep will be adjusting and the amount increasing.
- Your body's temperature will return to normal.
- Your energy may still be low but will be beginning to increase at this stage.
- Your skin will be hydrating regularly and will be looking and feeling clearer.
- Weighing yourself should be a distant memory. If it's not, zip back to Step 7, and refresh your memory of the importance of tossing those scales in the bin. Then tap on what's stopping you from freeing yourself from your scale chains?

As you take back control and learn to make peace with food, the anxiety and fears will subside further.

The compulsive and negative thoughts about food and your body reduce.

What emerges is a considerable amount of space for many wonderful things like more pleasant thoughts and actions that come in to replace the negativity that has been bubbling in your cauldron.

If you're struggling with a lack of enthusiasm at this stage, continue using the "Electrify Your Motivation" technique from Step 2, to ramp up your determination to continue along this positive pathway to freedom.

Month 4 to 6

- There are also many helpful aspects at this stage of your recovery. For example, you'll feel more positive thanks to the knowledge you've learned about restriction and how diets don't actually work!
- Bloating and water retention will have reduced. Your weight has evened out as your body adjusts to find its own natural setpoint.
- You have many encouraging positive changes as you learn more about your healing, and this makes you feel encouraged! You realize that your symptoms are all part of recovery, and everybody has them.
- Your triggers are still lurking, but your confidence to change; these continues to develop, as do your feelings and thoughts about your body image.
- You feel more empowered each day when you don't give in to your eating disorder and realize that you're actually on the stable pathway to recovery and a significant change is slowly taking place! You can now see the light clearly at the top of the dark hole.
- Your fear of foods is continuing to reduce as you start to enjoy eating, including different foods into your structured eating program. Now is definitely the time to reread Step

4, and begin with your intuitive eating plan if you haven't already done so.

- Your confidence will be flourishing as your social life increases.

7-8 months

- Your dark hole is lightening as you get closer to the top.
- Many people feel well on the way to permanent recovery, knowing what works for them and what to avoid.
- There still will be good and bad days, but it's not only about your weight or body-related fears; you now experience normal fluctuations of emotions.
- Your bloating and water retention may have reduced or disappeared completely.
- Confidence with your eating patterns is still increasing, and most of the time, you can eat like a normal person. (How incredible does that feel, making that dream a reality?)
- You become even more aware of feelings of hunger, only eating when you're hungry, slowly eating as you focus on the incredible tastes and flavors of your food.

You tune in to your feelings of contentment or knowing that you've had enough and you're at that moderately full stage and stop eating.

- Each day, you become more confident, accepting your body the way it looks.

9-12 months

- Oh my gosh, you'll now be reaching the top of the dark hole, you finally feel you're very close to recovering completely. Wahooo! You're incredible!
- Your urges to binge have diminished; you're nourishing your body and in control around foods.
- You continue to learn about your thoughts and feelings as unknown feelings are now brought to the surface, but you've learned how to experience them in positive ways. You no longer have that toxic leprechaun spouting his evil mutterings.

  Maybe now is the time to toss him back down the hole as you watch him fall down into the abyss.

- I'm not saying that you've recovered completely, but you're feeling incredibly healthy and eating like a normal person.

You now have all the knowledge, strength, and wisdom you need to keep you on this straight clear pathway. You have that sparkle back in your eyes. You're worthy of love and belonging, just as you are.

 **YOU ARE THE OTHER SIDE....**
I'M SO PROUD OF YOU

8. TOP TIPS ON HOW TO KEEP YOUR EMPOWERING MOTIVATION ERUPTING

We've talked about motivation to change now, but staying focused on this change sometimes is difficult.

What would help keep you on that motivational path? Ideas could be:

- So many people have overcome bulimia, so hop on the internet and read their success stories, blogs, Facebook, or in books.
- Many well-known celebrities overcome bulimia. Find one whom you admire and read their positive story. Keep that adrenalin of motivation pumping through your blood.
- Think about what motivates you explicitly to keep your focus clear. Imagine you're a volcano and that motivation just keeps erupting over and over to keep you moving forward.

HOW TO WIND UP YOUR MOTIVATION WITH THE "MOTIVATION BOOSTER" TECHNIQUE

In Step 6, you learned the exceptional skill of the "Spin and Win" technique to reduce your scared feelings about leaving your bulimia behind you. Remember, you can use that technique for any painful feeling you may be having at any time.

We're going to do something similar here to wind up your motivation as if it were an old-fashioned spinning top that you spin by pumping the handle on the top, and the longer you pumped, the faster it would spin. This will be you pumping up your motivation to really get you to move forward.

1. Imagine something that you're really motivated to do.

    It could be going on your idyllic vacation or signing the paperwork to buy your dream home. Visualize the scene, seeing it through your own eyes as though it's here and now; imagine what you would see and hear and feel exactly how being motivated feels. Once you have that motivation, spin this feeling inside you to intensify it.

2. Imagine yourself taking your first or second, third, fourth, fifth step in your recovery plan, see yourself doing so well, feeling so good, and being proud about yourself for taking control and finally making that decision to change. Again, visualize the scene, imagining what you would see, hear, and feel.

3. Spin the feeling of motivation faster and faster as you think about your step toward recovery.

4. Imagine again yourself taking your next step, see and feel how proud and delighted you are of yourself and spin that feeling.

5. Think about your next step again and follow through fantastically, feeling incredible with the feeling of motivation and spin that faster and faster.

Keep spinning for as long as you wish, and every time you aren't feeling motivated to go forward in life, re-run this technique to wind you up like that spinning top (Bandler, 2010).

Video Demonstration Link: https://bulimiasucks.com/motivation-booster/

9. **SEE NUMBER 8!** Keep winding up that motivation.

"EVERY TIME YOU ARE TEMPTED TO REACT IN THE SAME OLD WAY, ASK IF YOU WANT TO BE A PRISONER OF THE PAST OR A PIONEER OF THE FUTURE" - DEEPAK CHOPRA

10. AND FINALLY....

As you keep your motivation spinning every given moment of every day, it will empower you to stay clear of straying from your tantalizing new pathway to freedom.

 Your recovery is all about you and you and you! You are the number one priority in your life now. You deserve to recover.

RECOVERED - THIS IS WHO YOU WERE MEANT TO BE

The same you, but after all you've been through having had bulimia, robbing you of your true soul, you'll be different but in so many positive ways.

In recovery, as I mentioned earlier, everyone is different, and the length of time it takes you to recover is perfect for you as long as you stay focused and achieve recovery.

Think now how taking these 10 steps throughout this book will benefit not only you but also your family, friends, and people you don't even like! They'll all benefit.

All you have to do is make the decision to commit to your recovery, step outside of your comfort zone, and hold your own hand through each step.

You absolutely CAN achieve your dream of freedom from Bulimia

Wahooo! You've completed each step. Congratulations!

I wrote this book for you, with the incredibly powerful tools to change all the different areas in your life connected with your bulimia, to set you free and inspire and motivate you to stay focused on your new positive pathway. Nowwwww is the time to start to trust you're worth fighting for and enjoy the life you're entitled to live.

HOW TO CONTACT ME:

Bulimia can be painfully lonely, so come and join us on our Facebook page, "Bulimia Sucks!" https://www.facebook.com/groups/BulimiaSuck/.

It can be encouraging to connect with others who are going through the same experiences as you. Also, hear how others have overcome specific problems in their recovery.

How to find me:

Website Address: bulimiasucks.com

Email Address: katehudsonhall@gmail.com

I see clients on a one-to-one basis either in person or online via Skype, WhatsApp, Facetime, and other web-based services.

Jane Fonda (American actress)

Jane Fonda dealt with an eating disorder for decades, but she kept her bulimia a secret from the world. "I wasn't very happy from, I would say, puberty to 50? It took me a long time. It was in my 40s, and if you suffer from bulimia, the older you get, the worse it gets. It takes longer to recover from a bout," she told *Harper's Bazaar* in a 2011 interview. "I had to make a choice: I live, or I die," and she said she decided to "fill that empty space with something" (Firman, 2020).

CONCLUSION

Wahay, now you know how to reprogram your mind to continue to guide you forward through your recovery powerfully.

If you've only read the book once, now is your time to take yourself back to step 1 and begin to slowly learn how you're going to completely turn your life around. Then work through all your negative behaviors, links, and habits.

If you've worked methodically through the book. Fantastic. Now, take yourself back through the book regularly to refresh your mind with the variety of techniques. To then run through them to further cement the foundations of your pathway to full recovery.

Throughout the book, you've been shown incredible tools and techniques to help guide you through your recovery.

So, let's recap on what you've learned in each step...

Step 1. Here, you read about the differences between bulimia and anorexia and the possible causes of your bulimia. You also learned about NLP and submodalities then used them in the "New You" technique. So, keep stepping into that new you and absorb all the powerful thoughts and feelings regularly.

Step 2. You learned all about your bulimic cycle and how your triggers cause your urges. Then the "Instant Trigger Change" technique to powerfully change how you react to your triggers. Then your first motivational booster with the powerful "Electrify Your Motivation" technique.

Step 3. You broke down the big picture of your bulimic cycle to understand how your behaviors are linked to your urges. Then you worked with the space between your urges and binges, sitting in that space and then working with urge surfing, riding with the urge to loosen its grip and begin to see and feel it dissolve.

Step 4. In this step, you were introduced to your structured eating program. To begin to re-balance your body and reverse the effects of malnutrition and created your structured eating program.

You also learned about intuitive eating and how to:

- Only eat when you're hungry
- Reap the benefits of eating slowly and consciously
- Tune into your feelings of satisfaction or "knowing" that you've had enough and stop eating

Step 5. Here you learned how powerful your imagination is and the huge benefits of using it positively. We looked at what causes you to be stressed and then moved onto your limiting beliefs. Then you learned the excellent tool of the "Thought-Stopping" technique. To free your mind of this never-ending droning leprechaun!

Step 6. In this step, you found answers to the multitude of feelings connected to being scared of all the changes you're making. The more information you learn about it, the easier it is to move forward.

By reading about your scared feelings, you learned the incredible "Spin and Win" technique. To address any feelings of being scared, panicky, worthless, hopeless, and all the other beastly feelings you may be having. Keep going; it works. In fact, they all work!

Step 7. As you become more aware of your habit cycle, it will be easier to address the old habits and create new empowering habits that work for you. Especially with the "Shatter That Habit" technique.

Step 8. In this step, you learned the unique, effective tapping technique, so wherever you are in life, you have the immediate tool to reduce any tricky thoughts or feelings you may have. Excellent.

Step 9. In this step, you learned about the different therapies that you can research to find the right one for you. Plus, the benefits of supplements.

Step 10. In this step, you learned the importance of visualization and goal setting. Also, what will happen throughout your recovery time-line. Plus, another powerful motivational booster to empower you to keep you on track to your full permanent recovery.

AND FINALLY

An empowering suggestion for you right now

Remember the unbelievably powerful suggestion I was given at age 17 from step 1 and one of the reasons why I ended up down this same dark hole you're in right now?

Well, the suggestion I'm going to give you right here and now is:

**All your negative behaviors, habits, and patterns
you've learned can also be... UNLEARNED.**

NEED MORE HELP THROUGH YOUR RECOVERY?

If you would like more help in your journey to freeing yourself completely of bulimia, then come join us on:

"Bulimia Sucks!" Facebook Page

Bulimia can be painfully lonely, so come and join us on our Facebook page, "Bulimia Sucks!" It can be so encouraging to connect with others going through the same experiences as you and hear how others have overcome specific problems in their recovery at https://www.facebook.com/groups/BulimiaSuck/.

How to find me:

Website Address: bulimiasucks.com

Email Address: katehudsonhall@gmail.com

I see clients on a one-to-one basis either in person or online via Skype, WhatsApp, Facetime, and other web-based services.

This is what you can expect to happen when you contact me:

Depending on how you contact me, initially, I like to speak to my client in person on the dog and bone (that's the phone if you're not a cockney Londoner!), and if that isn't possible, then we connect via email, and from there, we would make the first initial appointment. I would then send you a questionnaire and diary to complete and return to me before our first appointment in person or online. It's as easy as that!

Please see my other books:

Bulimia Sucks! Personal Workbook:
https://amzn.to/3z914qU

Bulimia Sucks! Personal Food Journal:
https://amzn.to/3AeET39

Bulimia Sucks! Audiobook:
https://amzn.to/3sUZhmS

Bulimia Sucks! Coloring Book:
https://amzn.to/3axWVBZ

REFERENCES

Bandler, R. (2010). *Get the life you want*. HarperElement

Bandler, R., Roberti, A, & Fitzpatrick, O. (2013). The ultimate introduction to NLP: How to build a successful life. HarperCollins

Barnes, Z. (2015, February 25). Inspiring Quotes From 7 Celebs Who've Struggled with Eating Disorders. *Women's Health*. https://www.womenshealthmag.com/life/g19957616/celebs-who-fought-eating-disorders/

Brown West-Rosenthal, L. (2016, August 29). Spice Girl Geri Halliwell reveals she battled bulimia. Shape. https://admin.web.shape.com/celebrities/news/spice-girl-geri-halliwell-reveals-she-battled-bulimia

Craig, G., & Craig, T. (n.d.). How to do the EFT tapping basics - The basic recipe. https://www.emofree.com/nl/eft-tutorial/tapping-basics/how-to-do-eft.html

Eating Recovery Center. (2017, April 26.) 22 celebrities speak out about eating disorders and body positivity. [blog]. https://www.eatingrecoverycenter.com/blog/april-2017/23-celebrities-speak-out-about-eating-disorders-and-body-positivity

Firman, T. (2020, February 19). 30 celebrities get real about what it's like to live with an eating disorder. *Prevention*. https://www.prevention.com/health/health-conditions/g30996694/celebrities-with-eating-disorders/?slide=13

Kass, A. E., Kolko, R. P., & Wilfley, D. E. (2013). Psychological treatments for eating disorders. *Current Opinion in Psychiatry, 26*(6), 549–555. https://doi.org/10.1097/YCO.0b013e328365a30e

Mason, M. (2017, August 23). Prince William has candidly opened up about his mum's battle with bulimia. *Marie Claire*. https://www.marieclaire.co.uk/news/celebrity-news/princess-diana-eating-disorder-531800

Mayo Clinic. (n.d.) Bulimia: Overview. https://www.mayoclinic.org/diseases-conditions/bulimia/symptoms-causes/syc-20353615

Olivares, C. (2014, July 02). Nicole Scherzinger opens up about battling bulimia. *Shape*. https://www.shape.com/celebrities/nicole-scherzinger-opens-about-battling-bulimia

Pearl, D. (2020). 29 stars who battled eating disorders—and came out strong. *People*. https://people.com/health/celebrities-who-had-eating-disorders/

ACKNOWLEDGMENTS

I would like to dedicate this book to all of the incredible people who have inspired me to write this book, especially:

Cousin Emily, who told me, "You can do it."

Judith, my accountability buddy, for her encouragement and extraordinary intuitive inspiration

Reginald, or is it Lorenzo? For his "word" and not words help

Jane (Jakie) for her honesty, support, AND inspirationally leading me up the garden path, which always ends up in a puff of malarkey

Louise and her phenomenal motivation and belief in me

Antionette for her methodical eye for perfection, love, and support

Lulu for her experience or was it all a dream? Also, our inspiring mission in life!

Linda for her valuable words of wisdom

Cousin Karen for being like a sister to me and all of her never-ending miraculous support

My Goddaughter Kate, for her ingenious artistic talent

Winibush for her enthusiasm for encouragement

Gil for her generous guidance and knowledge

Neil for his huge wealth of knowledge and positive inspiration

Mark in leprechaun land, for his extraordinary words

Clare for her fine toothcomb editing skills

Nichola, because you <u>WILL break free</u>

Marcy for her nourishment of encouragement and motivation

My editor Wayne Purdin, for all his help, advice, guidance, and wealth of knowledge, plus for not telling me this is a load of twaddle!

And finally, for those with bulimia, stay focused on your pathway to freedom. AND because you CAN do this.

"REMEMBER TO DOWNLOAD YOUR TWO BONUS FREEBIES"

As a huge thank you for investing in my book, I have created you a:

FAMILY & FRIENDS SUPPORT EBOOK DOWNLOAD

So, when you are ready for that help and encouragement from your loved ones, download and send them the mini ebook to learn positive tips to support you in your recovery.

CLICK HERE TO SIGN UP FOR YOUR FREE FAMILY & FRIENDS SUPPORT EBOOK DOWNLOAD

https://bulimiasucks.com/support-e-book/

PLUS THERE'S MORE...

A DYNAMIC BULIMIA SUCKS! HYPNOSIS RECORDING DOWNLOAD

This powerful relaxation hypnosis recording will guide your unconscious mind to reprogram your bulimic behaviors so that you will change the way you are thinking and feeling and motivate you towards your goal of freedom from bulimia.

It's best to listen to this recording when you have 40 minutes to relax, let go and allow your unconscious mind to absorb all the powerful suggestions. Enjoy!

WARNING: Please do not listen to this recording while driving, operating heavy machinery, or if you have epilepsy or clinical depression.

CLICK HERE TO DOWNLOAD YOUR FREE POWERFUL MP3 BULIMIA SUCKS! HYPNOSIS DOWNLOAD

https://bulimiasucks.com/bulimia-recording/

ABOUT THE AUTHOR

At the age of 18, I began my bulimic career in earnest. Fifteen years later and after much help. I eventually freed myself from the clutches of anorexia and bulimia. I then stepped out and decided to take a different bulimic pathway. Feeling the great need to help others as I had been helped. I then trained as a psychotherapist, hypnotherapist, and NLP practitioner.

I have spent the last two decades working as an eating disorder therapist. With all my experience, learnings, and knowledge, in 2019 decided to write a book on how to reprogram the mind to overcome bulimia. Teaching my powerful "Bulimia Sucks! Program" has incredible tools and techniques to break bulimia behavioral patterns permanently.

Living and working in London. It's a wonderful escape to spend summers enjoying the views from the middle of a field on my land in Cornwall overlooking the Atlantic ocean.

While writing this memoir of my own experiences with the beast, or I should say bulimia! I still have a clear picture of what I went through and the memory of the horrific feelings I felt. But what's interesting to me is that, yes, I have those memories, but it's entirely in my past. Now there's never even a thought of bingeing and purging. My leprechaun is extinct!

I eat healthily, run three times a week, and have been at the same weight for 20 years. Well, apart from three pregnancies! But I naturally slipped back to my original weight before each pregnancy. (Remember your body's natural set point?)

So honestly, if I can break free from bulimia without any specific methods. Then you, with all the incredibly powerful techniques in this book, can too.

CAN YOU HELP?

Thank You for Reading My Book!

I really appreciate all of your feedback,
and I love hearing your thoughts.

So, I need your input to make the next version of this
book and my future books even more empowering.

Please leave me an honest review on Amazon; oh yes, I
would love to know what you thought of the book.

Thank you so much!

Kate Hudson-Hall

P.S. Rover, my fluffyness in this image did help to keep me
sane while writing this book. Hense the claim; it's his book!

Printed in Great Britain
by Amazon

44199744R00188